VAN HALEN
Jumpin' for the dollar

John Shearlaw

Exclusively Distributed
In North America By
Cherry Lane Books
PORT CHESTER, NY 10573

Whilst every effort has been made to trace and contact
the photographers of all the pictures in some cases it was
impossible. The publishers would be grateful to hear
from any photographers who have not been credited.

First published in Great Britain in 1984 by Zomba
Books, Zomba House, 165–167 Willesden High Road,
London NW10 2SG.

Cherry Lane Books, Port Chester, NY 10573,
New York, USA

© John Shearlaw, 1984.

ISBN 0 946391 51 3.

All rights reserved. No part of this book may be repro-
duced in any form or by any means, except for the
inclusion of brief quotations in a review, without prior
permission in writing from the Publisher.

Designed by Jim Reader

Cover Designed by The Fish Family

Production Services by Book Production Consultants,
Cambridge

Typeset by Wenden Typesetting Services Ltd, Wenden
Court, Wendens Ambo, Saffron Walden, Essex.

Printed by Bemrose Printing C.I.P., Derby

First edition.

Everything is true once it is written, somebody once said, and I've no reason to disbelieve that worthy sentiment . . . even now. Suffice to say that all published sources have been credited where necessary; and to all those that have taken on Van Halen (in whatever form) and lived you have my written thanks and indebtedness.

For special thanks I have to mention Nick Kent (once of the NME) and Oui magazine for inspiration in the UK and US respectively, Martin at WEA for being a fan as well as an employee, Mark Cooper, Dave Walters, Dave 'Monster' Jarrett, Chris Welch, Alan Jones (for the facts and figures), Peter Hogan, Lorraine Johnston, Gillian Bigelou, Mic Cheetham, Brigid McConville (the only one who really knows why), Keith Drinkwater and everyone else at Castle Donington.

Thanks also to David Lee Roth, Michael Anthony, Edward Van Halen and Alex Van Halen (plus a crew of God knows how many millions) for making the whole fantasy come to life. Whether we meet on the psycho's couch or on the backstage coach — some time, some day — it was a lot of fun.

JOHN SHEARLAW
August 1984

"It's only rock 'n' roll . . .   (The Rolling Stones)

"Rock 'n' roll is more than music . . .
(David Lee Roth)

"On top of the Crumpetty Tree
The Quangle Wangle sat,
But his face you could not see,
On account of his Beaver Hat.
For his Hat was a hundred and two feet wide,
With ribbons and bibbons on every side
And bells, and buttons, and loops, and lace,
So that nobody ever could see the face
Of the Quangle Wangle Quee."
(Edward Lear)

"The trouble with most folks isn't so much their ignorance, as knowing so many things that ain't so."
(Josh Billings, with apologies to H. L. Mencken)

● David Lee Roth; 'My love keeps lifting me . . .'

Contents

Foreword	6
1. Then and now . . .	7
2. How the West was won — California 1973–1978.	10
3. Over-sexed, underpaid and over here — The UK 1978–1980.	26
4. Good evening Columbus (or should that be Cleveland?) — The US 1979–1983.	41
5. Fact and faction — 1978–1984 *A Van Halen Miscellany.*	50
6. Off and on — the music 1978–1984.	67
7. Jump! — The world 1983–1984.	73
8. David Lee Roth — Myth, Ms. and mastery.	83
9. Until the next time . . .	89
Discography.	95

Foreword

'Van Halen — Jumpin' For The Dollar' is what should really be called An Aprocryphal Tale. Truly it is a modern folk tale — even if it is about rock 'n' roll (which is perhaps the whole point).

Rest assured every fact is true . . . as long as you are prepared to perceive that is the case.

• *Whaddya mean, no teeth?*

Van Halen are public property; anything that isn't here is up for you to provide.

And don't forget to tell your friends!

1. Then and now...

In a nutshell Van Halen are four musicians from varying backgrounds who came together in California in the early seventies. After slogging out four years (or five, or six) on the bar band circuit they acquired a record deal, and since 1978 have pushed out six albums, each one of them going platinum in the States, and each one outselling its predecessor. The last, at the time of writing, was '1984', which also spawned the band's first US number one single, 'Jump'.

They're also in the Guinness Book Of Records as the highest paid band for any one performance; and although this will eventually be superseded Van Halen certainly won't.

Van Halen are a band who've created their own legend on little more than hard work, a little inspiration, a lot of noise and (in more ways than one) absolutely superb timing.

Their story is a fairy tale, or as academics would have it, an urban folk tale. Its shortened version has been repeated so often, as are all good fables, that it is undeniably seen to be true. Van Halen have done nothing to change it. To them the credo that Van Halen are "the biggest hard rock band in America" is as true as any number of other credos that Americans believe. Many of these could be applied to Van Halen. To wit: "The best songs occur to composers when they are doing something inconsequential like showering or making love and only take twenty minutes or so to reach their final form"; "If somebody doesn't speak your language you must shout at him to be understood"; "The human race is the only species that is sexually active the whole year long"; "History is destined to repeat itself". And "Spread is an inevitable consequence of middle age".

All of these apply somewhere in the narrative and all, of course, are nonsense. But so too is rock 'n' roll. Any other way it wouldn't be much fun. Van Halen proved that a long time ago, and look ready to keep proving it right through the eighties.

To many Van Halen is a synonym for crass, unbearable or simply bullshit. To a great many more they are a cathartic release from modern America. Born in the fifties, teenagers in the seventies, and fully fledged rock stars in the eighties, they are a truly digestible, living and breathing phenomenon. Life wouldn't be the same without them.

After all, in many ways, Van Halen are public property. How you choose to use them, how they

● *Bellbottoms and boots – pre 1980.*

choose to use you, is a matter of personal taste and speculation. From those who first picked up on Van Halen back in '73, to those who copped on to the first album, to those who only know them as the band who made 'Jump' there is something to be gained from the story. It even has a happy ending.

Two views, one public and one private, can set the ball rolling. From then on in it's Van Halen's very own freeway. First Gillian Bigelou, friend, Californian, a one-time fan (born in the same year as David Lee Roth and also shares the same star sign) comments: "First of all in California, then right across America, Van Halen were always there, or going to be

- ABOVE: *'Irene, goodnight, Irene'* – *the end of the show.*
- RIGHT: *Edward the vain Knight.*

there. Going to see them was something that everybody did at least once, no matter what they felt about it afterwards. You didn't rationalise it, say they were non-gay, non-black, non-punk or junk like that. They were there, like high school and hot dogs."

Second David Lee Roth, just for now the presidium and mouthpiece for the other three members of Van Halen (Edward Van Halen, Alex Van Halen and Michael Anthony): "I think there is evidence that Van Halen has changed the face of rock music in two ways. One, because half the musicians try to copy the band. They grow their hair and play guitar lickety-split like Edward and they try to imitate Alex's drum sound. Two, because the other half is so revolted by our music and our pose and the way I do interviews that they're forced to come up with alternatives. Either way it seems we've effected some kind of change."

Whether they'll continue doing so isn't even considered here (not even at the end, if you get that far). A story is a story, and as far as Van Halen's goes, his is a legend.

2. How the West was won — California 1973–1978

● ABOVE: *The Dionysius meets the Dutchman . . . musically speaking.*

One of the oldest stories that Americans believe and know to be true is that the whole stinking rich, sunshine-kissed, coke-coddled and crime ridden 'golden' state of California will one day slide into the Pacific Ocean — taking part of the American Dream with it but leaving life under the Stars and Stripes largely undisturbed.

Another theory, for which any bookmaker will give you a great deal better odds, is that the infamous Los Angeles smog will one day reach such intolerable levels that life, as West Coasters know it, will cease to exist. Rioting, looting and arson will engulf the city (and eventually the State) leaving a trail of destruction far more damaging than the relatively more normal exigencies posed by the geological instability of the San Andreas fault.

Of course, both events could occur simultaneously. I'd prefer to think not. No, a much better betting proposition is that on that particular day Van Halen will be playing rock 'n' roll somewhere in the world.

California made Van Halen, but it'll never break them. "The world of rock 'n' roll is not five nights in LA," David Lee Roth once said, "It's nights in Ioline, San Antonio, Buffalo and Bristol, England." He'll stay true to his word. As California destructs Van Halen will still be espousing its values somewhere else. Even if Pasadena — "our own backyard," as Dave always describes it — goes it'll be remembered in a Van Halen song; probably played at

• *Bourbon and bass, beef and bare, LA 1984.*

maximum volume at Bridlington Spa, England, or Cherry Hill, New Jersey.

That's why Van Halen are popular beyond belief. They met in California, they've taken its rock 'n' roll values, and whether it be through the lens of a Nikon F-1, a 100,000 watt stack of Marshall amps, or the headphones of a Sony Walkman, given them back to the world.

The early Van Halen story may have elements of formula and elements of fluke and maybe even farce, but they're still playing true to their word. And to their world as they perceived it. They wanted to make money — they are now enormously rich. They wanted to play rock 'n' roll — they still do. The words of the old song spring to mind — "California, here I come!". If they hadn't gone there they wouldn't have made it. And if that sounds like part of a fairy story . . . it is.

Alex Van Halen was born in the spring of 1955 in the small Dutch town of Nijmegen, the son of a professional musician. His brother Edward followed some eighteen months later. Both were encouraged to "learn music" at an early age. Their father suggested the clarinet or the saxophone, the tools of his trade, but it was mother who won. "My mother thought if we were going to get into music it should be something respectable so we both had piano lessons," said Edward later. "It started when I was six but the only thing I didn't like was that you had to learn everything by the book. Still, I guess it helped my ears . . . and my fingers."

Alex, still cited as "the rock drummer who can read music" by more than one critic, had happier memories. "When the Beatles first came out we cut out little cardboard guitars and jumped up and down. We thought it was fun. But there comes a time when you have to work for it or it's just a dream . . ."

At that time there were other dreams for the Van Halen family. As legend has it the parents were encouraged by letters from relatives about the 'dream life' in California. Stuff about picking oranges from trees and a good climate. So in the mid sixties the Van Halens upped and moved to Pasadena. "Everything we'd heard was a crock of shit," Edward later recalled in one of his blacker moods. But it was the real start. Things happened in California. "If I hadn't have started playing rock 'n' roll I'd have been pumping gas," said Edward in 1979, more than ten years on.

In America of course the fairy tale was by that time well under way. The cardboard guitars had been replaced by real instruments, and the piano lessons were over. Alex strummed away on an acoustic guitar

● LEFT: *Roth singing somewhere over the Rainbow.*

while Eddie borrowed the money to buy a drum kit: "I suppose it was the Dave Clark Five that inspired me."

Again the legend takes over. Alex and Edward didn't fight (they probably did), but instead just swopped their instruments. "He could play 'Wipe Out' on the drums and I couldn't so we changed over," Edward was later quoted as saying. The early teens were spent at Pasadena High School, and musically the brothers were following their own separate idols, yet at the same time steadfastly playing together. "I'd study all Clapton's solos on the Cream albums at 16rpm," said Eddie. "Alex was into Ginger Baker." The brothers got older, Cream faded into a distant memory (although the influences remained along with the new ones: "I grew up with them all, Clapton, Beck, Page" — Eddie), and the brothers defied their grade difference and started a group.

For their own closely guarded reasons Edward and Alex always played together. And, apart from the odd excursion, have always done so since. "Alex is the only drummer I know," Eddie put it quite plainly some time later. "We seem to be able to work things out together ... I don't know why." The brothers traded riffs and rows simultaneously, but stuck it out. They had a group and "the only thing we wanted to do was rock". California was beginning to take over.

David Lee Roth thought so too. Only a few scant months, and 8000 miles, separated the arrival of the infant Roth from the infant Alex. David was born in 1955 in Bloomington, Indiana, the son of a successful surgeon. It's hardly surprising that Van Halen's front man has made more of his early past than the brothers, or indeed the self-effacing Michael Anthony. From the first 'real' interview in 1978 right through to more recent times, his entry into the legend, the fledgling fairy tale, has largely been unaltered. The story remains the same, and it's one that anchors Van Halen to reality.

"The old man, of course, wanted me to go to school," David states. "I had nine aunts and uncles on the old man's side and they're all doctors, except for one aunt who's a lawyer and one uncle, Uncle Manny who owned a club in Greenwich Village called the Cafe Wha. He was always into music and it was him who put his brothers and my aunt through

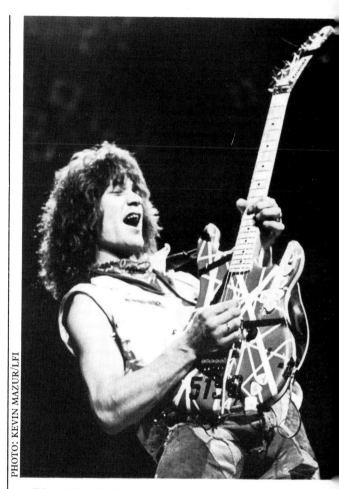

● *Edward Van Halen: a fret to society?*

school so there was never much dissension when I got around to saying I wanted to get into music. There were rows of course, but I said: 'The hell with this, I want to travel, I want to see the world, I want to get high while I'm doing it.' My parents wanted me to finish school, every parent does. They say you've got to have something to fall back on. 'Wait till you're 32 and then you can do it' they'd say.

"My family never supported me at all. It drove them wild that I could be thinking about making a living out of rock 'n' roll. You know the routine — "Show business? There's no future in it, it's the most vile, shark-infested water you can sail in" and so on. But I was determined.

"It goes back to when I was eight or nine or so.

They said I was hyperactive and sent me down to child guidance clinic."

At nine years old, the story goes, David was given a radio by Uncle Manny. The first record he claims he ever heard on the radio was 'Crying Time'. "It was years later I found out it was by Ray Charles but I knew then that I really and truly wanted to be a singer," Dave has told every interviewer who's ever asked him since 1978. "I didn't know what kind of singer, I kind of remember wanting a brass section but that stopped when I was eleven, I just knew I was going to do it. I didn't know it would be a rock 'n' roll band, but it was all there."

What followed was five years of what David now calls "social maladjustment". He had cropped hair at twelve years old, ("greased back so I could stand on my head on the pavement and impress the other guys"), he cracked his head on a farm tool (the scar is still there), he didn't go to school, he toyed with the idea of becoming a new Errol Flynn and he carried on singing. At 16 he was in California, in Pasadena. The notion of finishing school was still there, but the lure of the West Coast was even greater. "I cut class and lay out in the sun and carried on enjoying myself," he said. A year later, a few miles across town from the Van Halen brothers, he joined a group.

Michael Anthony, enigmatic, free thinking, free willed, was born in Chicago in 1955. By the age of seventeen he too had hauled his not inconsiderable talents in the direction of the Golden State. A self starter, an early leader . . . and the fourth to follow the lure, he started his own group.

★ ★ ★ ★

Years later David Lee Roth came up with the classic line: "People say to me 'You're from California, man, why don't you sound like the Eagles?' Crap! It was never like that. We sounded like Van Halen right from the beginning, even when we weren't playing Van Halen songs."

Give or take a year or two he was right. True, there were plenty of fledgling Eagles about (and whatever happened to them?) but even more of the kids were pounding it out on whatever they could lay their hands on. It was all about noise and getting noticed — California style.

Edward and Alex started the ball rolling with a heavy rock trio, which with ambition beyond their years they called Mammoth. Heavy, and not at all humble. Eddie, more interested in the guitar, nevertheless took the early singing role. Michael Anthony was poached from a rival group to beef up the bass sound.

"They put me through everything they could think when I first auditioned with them," Michael later recalled. "Chord changes, key changes and every damn thing. Somehow I survived and they said: 'Do you want to join our group?' I just kind of muttered 'Yeah', and that was it."

David Lee Roth, meanwhile, had taken to Pasadena like a duck to water and was extending his vocal range — and his potential sex appeal — in a group called the Redball Jets. "The name alone should indicate how authoritative our sound was," he said. "The music was garbage, but what a good time!" Rumour has it he had a good suntan, rapidly growing blond hair and what was amounting to more than a passable scream. Maybe Eddie heard it halfway across town.

David had certainly heard of Mammoth. "What they were playing wasn't really singing songs," he later said. "They'd do Black Sabbath covers and these verbatim Cream renditions that were note for note." But there was a musical power behind Mammoth that David recognised. A solid background for his own shouting and pouting. A ready made backline for a guy that could get people to look at *him*.

That early chemistry, forged in high school, is still there today. Fate . . . or fairy tale?

Within six months Roth had dumped the Jets and joined forces with Mammoth. It was 1973 and only two things have changed since — the name and the music. The first was easy, although one student acquaintance remembers the foursome once playing under the gruesome handle of 'Rat Salade'. However, a few late nights and a few six-packs got them comfortably settled as Van Halen.

The music took a little longer. And it was the time and the place that had a lot to do with it. California, a musical melting pot, and to most people then the place where the great American revival was taking place. Especially if you were young, white and wanted to play rock 'n' roll.

The revolutionary fervour surrounding America's involvement in Vietnam was being quietly forgotten. Slogans like "What are we fighting for?" were replaced by the motto, "Let's get down and party!"

Mark Cooper, who first saw Van Halen in 1975,

remembers the time: "It was a society based on forgetting everything that had gone before. The soft-bellied corrupt society was the new cliché and everybody wanted to be in there enjoying it. Southern California was the place to be."

"Socal" life was easy. "It was all about fast cars, kickin' ass and fucking," says one contemporary. "All you needed was sun, beer, a nice body and somebody to fuck with, or even just fuck around with." Another key word was movement: "Kids were maniacally into movement, like, let's get out and GO! Let's do it! It could be a surfboard, a skateboard, a car — fuck it, let's go now! If you were young and ready it was all there — racist, rich and rapacious somebody once said about it, but it was true."

"For most people it was a case of always being hot to party, preferably without an idea in your brain," says a survivor. "It was an animal instinct, but not a beastly one. I can remember the shorts, the long hair, frisbees and dope . . . and quaaludes if you really wanted to fall over. Mindless golden nihilism, no politics, no hassles, and fun at all costs."

"Socal" country was Van Halen country, and they made the most of it. How could you party without music? California was going through the laid-back late sixties and early seventies and was swinging back towards rock 'n' roll.

• *Dave plays goose the guitarist – and what an effect!*

- *Alex hides his Harley under the pit.*

It was a curious time. Memories of Led Zeppelin, Deep Purple and even Grand Funk Railroad were still there (Boston were huge and they owed something to all three). But there was a new spirit among the younger LA rockers. One contemporary called it "Wham, glam and thank you man." You played loud, you dressed up, and you tried to get noticed and get laid — in either order.

David Lee Roth was becoming a classic already. Maybe he had done his homework after all? Looking like he could have been born in Santa Barbara rather than the Mid West he had everything an up coast surfer would have been proud of — good teeth, long hair and a suntan. He was fit, and he was not afraid to flaunt it.

Van Halen needed him and he needed them. Eddie, looking impossibly young, was steering Van Halen towards hard rock, ably backed by Michael and Alex. David Lee Roth was steering people towards Van Halen.

This American hybrid — not a native Californian amongst them! — began to make waves in their adopted home. They absorbed a lot; the power and the postures of their rock 'n' roll peers and more than a bit of the posing.

If they started off playing everything and anything — and they did — somewhere along the line it began to sound like Van Halen. "Rock, hard rock, heavy rock, glam rock, heavy metal, call it what you like, was essential," I was told by one girl who lived in Pasadena in the mid seventies. "It was a good substitute for fucking like rabbits. It was even better if you could do both. Van Halen were *our* band for a while . . ."

Eddie, Alex, Michael and Dave never had a formula as such, but the mixture was there and the place was right. Their rehearsals were gigs — wherever they could get them — and the music started off as what people wanted to hear. But behind it all was a determination to make what people wanted to hear have one name only — Van Halen. In three years of solid work they turned the tables and were pulling in 3000 people for gigs at the Pasadena Civic Auditorium.

"The way we started was playing here, there and everywhere, like weddings," Dave told *Teenage Depression* magazine. "No kidding, we played a wedding where the people were over thirty ranging to 'You Really Got Me'. maybe sixty. When we got there they gave us the dirtiest looks, you know, because of the haircuts — what haircuts? — okay the lack of haircuts. They were all family of the bride and groom but I tell you by the end of the evening they were all jumping around and even asking for our songs by title like 'Runnin' With The Double' (that's 'Runnin' With The Devil' which we'd written) and 'Somebody Get Me A Datsun', and that was 'Somebody Get Me A Doctor'!"

Dave was always spokesman; a natural role on stage and off (even now). But there was something there that needed the four of them. Van Halen started out as a living jukebox, a party tape that moved (and maybe went to bed with the hostess afterwards). But as their repertoire increased — "Van Halen can play over two hundred songs, you'd be surprised at what we can do and what might turn up," Eddie was to say later — so did the power of each individual talent.

They didn't yet have the money for the volume but the guitar, bass and drums, somehow held together. And with Dave wailing away up front, they had style, variety and pulling power. And that came with three years of playing endless small clubs up and down the LA basin; bars, backyard parties, surfer's nights out, dance contests and even fields in the San Fernando Valley.

"The power of Van Halen comes from the club days," said Dave. "We used to play everything from ZZ Top to KC and the Sunshine Band. You should hear Van Halen playing 'Get Down Tonight'! We had to cover all the parts with guitar and vocals; we had to learn."

The input was huge, and gradually the new material started to come out. Eddie and Alex came up with the music, Dave with the words. In between, all the rest of the material, from Led Zeppelin downwards was, as one early fan puts it: "Van Halenised, you began to realise it was them playing, not some garage

• *Early daze; Eddie the best newcomer.*

band cranking out someone else's hits. They had style, and they were pushy."

And they were getting off on the fun. "It was never for the money. At heart it was always, how much do you want to play? And we wanted to play a whole lot," David told Oui magazine. "We got up on stage and misbehaved, and *then* we made it into a living.

"We loved those early days — the bars and the wet T-shirt gigs. For a while we were the Rock Corporation of LA and we did the very first wet T-shirt contests of in Southern California — the ones that got me busted and actually made it to the court trials. It was a great scene. I'd be the MC, with the band behind me, and I'd interview the contestant. 'What do you do for a living?' 'Oh, I'm a doughnut waitress from Canoga Park.' Then I'd make a joke and she'd jump into the pool and get wet. Then I'd say 'What song would you like to hear?' 'Oh, I'd just love 'Free Ride'.'

"So I'd have to say 'It seems this lady would love a free ride' and the audience would crack up. We'd play the song, she'd do her twitch and bump, and the rest of the girls would bounce in.

"At the end the judges are too fucked up to make any decision so we have to run through all the contestants again. 500 people standing on top of each other, drunk and screaming. And then there was the dance contests. Well, that's how you develop your habits and your attitudes as a band.

- ABOVE LEFT: *No flies, and flying high.*
- ABOVE: *Michael Anthony, 'the solid sender'.*
- RIGHT: *Van Halen in 'toilet talk' horror!*

"And you take them with you . . ."

Right again. The party might have started early but the hosts were aiming to be up all night. The Valley Girls and the zonked-out guys came along first — the famous guests came later.

First there was the Los Angeles Times, actually reviewing an unsigned band not once, but three times. Then Gene Simmons of Kiss — a real break this — appearing without make-up and with enough money to finance a demo tape. In the legend Gene talked about getting a manager and a deal, "some backing for the band". In reality they didn't. This was 1976. Two years later Gene Simmons got a "Special thanks to . . ." credit on the first Van Halen album, a credit that made heavy metal fans on both sides of the Atlantic sit up and take notice. Not bad for a walk on part.

The demo was part cover, part originals, part successful. And the party went right on through the winter, right through until a miserable February evening at the Starwood Club in South Hollywood. This time it *was* a Monday night and Van Halen were playing for free. The Starwood was 'up 'n' coming' territory — sweat your balls off and hope somebody

● *'If you want me, you only have to ask'.*

notices. Kids hung out in the car park, smoked dope, drank beer. Some of them even watched the band. But the Starwood was important. If the big wheels of the music business didn't exactly flock there in droves they would take a drive downtown if there was a nudge that there was something happening. With Van Halen there definitely was. Maybe Gene Simmons had made a few phone calls. Maybe not.

Mo Ostin, chairman of Warner Brothers Records, took the trip that night, along with the label's Executive Producer Ted Templeman. Both impressed they started negotiations to sign Van Halen to Warners that same evening. "It was like a dream," Dave was reported as saying. "But it happened and our party got a whole lot better from then on."

History doesn't record what actually happened on the stroke of midnight that particular evening, or even whether a glass slipper fitting a particular foot had any part in the proceedings. But there it was — Van Halen had Southern California in one pocket and a record deal in the other. The rest of the world was going to be easy.

****

The Van Halen story wouldn't be a legend if that hadn't actually turned out to be the case. In many respects the group were already self-moulded, while Ted Templeman's career as a producer had placed him up in the ranks of the near superhuman. Triumphs with the Doobie Brothers and then with the Montrose debut album in 1973 (roundly pronounced by many as the second best hard rock/heavy metal debut album ever to appear; the same arbitrators, naturally enough, pronounce *Van Halen I* as the best) placed him as a mixing desk master with a foot in both camps. The ability to blend melody and mayhem suited both parties down to the ground. And it turned out it was just what America (and later Great Britain and Japan) needed at the time.

The recording of *Van Halen I* wasn't a long drawn out affair. The group moved all their gear, lock, stock and battalion, into Sunset Sound and thundered away; covers one minutes, originals the next.

What Templeman had spotted was that Van Halen had a unique quality; an ability to thunder and crash with the best of them — "Christ, everyone in California knew they were loud," said one observer — but

also an ability to keep it short and dynamic. Van Halen hit hard and then stopped. Then they hit you again even harder. At a time when so-called hard rock went on forever, and so-called soft rock seemed to go on forever (but actually only lasted three minutes) Van Halen were a refreshing change.

"We pioneered lots of things, and that was as a result of all of those years of work," David said later. "First off we were into short songs — Beatles style — with a hard rock sound. And then there were the cover versions.

"Nobody would believe that they worked until they heard them on the album. Then bang, every rock 'n' roll band is doing four minute songs and cover versions."

Templeman extracted the best from Van Halen. Dave wasn't the greatest singer in the world (even he knew that) but he screamed and yelled and got on down. By contrast Eddie was already a brilliant guitarist and the best that a producer could do was put him up there in front and let him do it.

The result was a raunchy party that got onto vinyl. Maybe, with all the elements there, somebody else might have made the album in about a year — and then got accused of faking it.

Such was Van Halen's spirit and Ted Templeman's skill that it took about four weeks. And as Eddie was to point out later, defensively perhaps, "overdubbing was minimal".

Dave *did* scream like that and Eddie *did* play that fast. Believe it?

"I used to love it when people came up to me and said: "You know that scream you do, you got that off Deep Purple," said Dave. "I laughed a lot and said, no — I got it off the Ohio Players."

The album was also meant to be a kick in the ass. Something for the old rock 'n' rollers, who were still churning it out, to take notice of. And also something that was an answer to what had been assimilated on the West Coast as New Wave (punk, as such, barely dented California; it was only the sanitised later version that Van Halen were fighting against). It succeeded on both counts.

Van Halen I surfaced with eleven tracks, almost a world record at a time when six tracks from any other metal monster outfit might have led to thoughts about making it a double album. Two were covers — Ray Davies' "You Really Got Me' to be released as the band's first single, and John Brim's 'Ice Cream

• *All mouths and trousers – V.H. in the eighties.*

Man' — the rest were credited to the band, all named.

The cover was brash and colourful; sweat and cymbals, flaming guitars, bare chests and leather trousers. David Lee Roth adorned the back, bending over with a two foot mane of hair and a pair of platform boots that might have come supplied with an altimeter as an additional feature. Much to Ted Templeman's satisfaction, Warner Brothers obvious pleasure and Edward Van Halen's later confessed surprise *Van Halen I* was an instant hit in America. It carried no grace or favour — "something between AOR and punk, it seems to have found a niche", one American critic rather lamely put it — but merely entered the Billboard Top 20 . . . and stayed there.

By the time the album had gone platinum Eddie Van Halen had been voted 'Best New Guitarist Of The Year' by *Guitar Player* magazine, David Lee Roth had worked out the first five years of the band's history and taken on the role of the group's mouthpiece and Van Halen were in the process of establishing their first real record in the rock 'n' roll book of world records — the longest ever continuous tour by any band. Not surprisingly they called it the 'Van Halen World Vacation'. Seemingly the supplies of beer and music were never going to run out . . .

★★★★

In many ways the germination of the famous 1978 'World Vacation' lay back in 1976. The party spirit was there, the band roles were established even then. But given that time, and a hit album, and a few dollar chips to lay on the table Van Halen were literally able to go out with the enviable tag of 'overnight successes'. They didn't exploit it, they didn't need to. And none of the hopped up kids hanging round Vine or Sunset worried worth a damn. Van Halen were white, non-political and young. And they'd nearly made it.

How Van Halen turned a backyard barbeque in the San Fernando Valley into a nationwide party is really the essence of the legend. There's snow in upstate New York, but it doesn't cost a hundred bucks a gram in the winter. There sure as hell ain't no surf in Chicago, nor is it always Saturday night in New Orleans. Van Halen were an acceptable substitute. The myth was established. For most critics it was a case of "from the back of a flat top trailer in a Hollywood parking lot to a 40,000 seater stadium in Cleveland in a few short months". It was rather like saying "from two lines on the back of a cigarette pack to the Booker Prize in three weeks flat" — simply unbelievable.

But this was rock 'n' roll, what was seen was believed. And what rock 'n' roll critic worth his or her salt would tip up in Pasadena anyway? Just let those headlines roll, *this* story is worth following up. And no-one knew that better than David Lee Roth, or indeed the other three, who were ready to work their butts off to get Van Halen up there in lights as the biggest rock 'n' roll group of all time. "Success?" Dave once snorted, "we ain't even started yet." And that was in 1982.

The 1978 campaign was a double-edged sword, a swamping of the media (usually under limp headlines like "Van Halen's Party Goes On" and "All Play And Little Work For Van Halen") combined with an all-out blitzkrieg playing across the world. "Van Halen is us, our music, our lives," said Dave. And off they went to prove it.

Behind the scenes there was the solid hard work — and money — that went into getting across the message that the album had sent across the airwaves. The assembly of a crew, a rig, lights and all the

● *Minimal guitar, maximum volume.*

razzamatazz necessary to keep them going for the best part of a year. Things like merchandising, a fan club, a logo, plenty of clothes, vitamins and Budweiser — and a large measure of self confidence.

In front of the scenes there was no problem. Dave probably summed it up best when *Rolling Stone* magazine (middle-aged by that time, but still influential) finally got around to recognising them. "We're not tasteless," he pronounced. "We may sing some raunchy songs but basically we've just got an energy that blazes you on, a real hard-driving, straight ahead, can't lose sound."

So far, so good. The interview was in New York

• *Dave as the Quangle Wangle.*

and Van Halen were supporting Journey. They didn't "Blow 'em off stage" as one fan (now retired) remembered it; they just did themselves, the album and their image a whole lot of good. This, after all, was a long way from Sunset.

David continued: "Van Halen is an attitude, like driving down the Strip with a load of girls, the radio on and a couple of cases of beer. We all have it, and when we get together it comes out in our music. We blow it out together. We take you and make you feel good, then we play another song and you feel like breaking something. It's a physical thrill, like the first seven minutes of a porno flick. We act out rock fantasies and it's all from our experience; the cars, the girls, the beer, the parties, the sweat and the fun. It's spontaneous combustion!"

Van Halen took it round the country — every night a Saturday night, you'd better believe it. Eddie wanted to play and play, and then play some more. Michael kept on playing, and when he stopped he kicked his bass guitar, picked it up and started playing some more. Alex's kit got bigger and his sound got louder. Dave screamed and sang and drank and fucked and talked. Van Halen hadn't really made it yet, but they were getting there. The fantasy was becoming reality.

Almost before the ink was dry on their visas for Britain, Europe and Japan, the band played in California as support to Black Sabbath, Boston and Sammy Hagar.

Dave told *Teenage Depression* magazine, and everyone else for years after: "Did you hear about the parachuting? We thought it would be great to parachute into the stadium which is what we did. It was great. We were scared to shit, but it worked. We landed in the parking lot. We had the best 'chutes with the Van Halen logo on them.

"Boston said 'You'll never do it' but we did man, we freaked 'em out. Ever seen 60,000 people faint at once?"

Ah, the legend! The story was repeated for years afterwards and, for many, even overshadowed the drink and drugs and sex and all night party mythology that was to become an integral part of the Van Halen story.

It was only in 1984 that Dave told the *Daily Mirror's* Robin Eggar that the whole thing was a hoax. "We hid in the back of a van for four and a half hours after hiring four paratroopers who wore long wigs," he said. "They dropped behind the stage and we rushed out of the van!"

Yet it worked at the time; that's rock 'n' roll. To all intents and purposes Van Halen had defied death and sky dived into their own backyard (and which story do you believe?). Their record company said they had done it and that was enough. By going back to California Van Halen had transcended themselves, it was their turn to call the shots. Next stop, the world. And after that, who'd say no to a party that has lasted for six years and still shows no signs of stopping?

Let the Brits have their say — David Lee Roth always did — and hear about the *real* triumphs later.

Like, there was punk and heavy metal and . . . was the music business really stagnating? As it turned out Van Halen timed their arrival to perfection.

• *'I think I can see what you're doing wrong'.*

3. Over-sexed, underpaid and over here — The UK 1978–1980

Great Britain in 1978 was, as most Americans put it, "a whole different ball game" musically speaking. A nation split asunder by punk, reggae, heavy metal, MOR, pop, rock and the remnants of every musical trend that had surfaced and made the charts since the Beatles in 1963.

The Sex Pistols were duped into singing 'Anarchy In The UK', and for a while punks roamed the streets of London (and sometimes even Basildon, Essex and other unlikely places) but as in most things in rock 'n' roll it was the lure of the pound that ruled the day. And all those years ago, the pound was at one of its highest points against the dollar than it ever had been.

There was no musical revolution, no overthrowing of idols — Fleetwood Mac nestled comfortably in the album charts alongside the Clash, Bob Marley and Status Quo — just a horde of new names and new faces clamouring for a record contract. Even if, like Elvis Costello, they had to busk outside a sales conference at a top London hotel to do it.

But, in some senses, it wasn't only rock 'n' roll. It was more than music. Peter York, a journalist who later wrote *Style Wars*, was one of the first to identify 'the tribes' that followed a particular style of music; even if the comforts of London kept him confined to the roots of gay disco, the survivors of "Swinging London', and the entirely unthreatening merger of punk into New Wave.

One such 'tribe' who survived a lot of things in the seventies that would have defeated even General

- BELOW: *'Thank you . . . (where the hell are we?)'*
- RIGHT: *'This one's for Quincy and Michael'*.

Custer at his tactical best, and carried their scars and totems right through until the eighties, were those who chose to follow heavy metal; by then an entirely acceptable term to its followers. They were guaranteed to brave mud and rain and potentially deafening volume in order to see their bands. They were usually male and they wanted to get drunk and get off on the music, and could usually be counted on to spend the last of their money on a T-shirt or a tour programme even if it meant hitching a hundred miles home in a downpour at 2am in the morning. They still do.

They also bought records. And for all the lambasting heavy metal fans received in Britain — and for a bored music press it was a lot — they were surprisingly quick to pick up on something new, exciting and different. Even better they could spot a fake a mile off. Punks were duped in 1978, while the average pop fan carried on blissfully unaware. Heavy metal fans, however, discovered new bands whilst remaining faithful to the old heroes.

Between 1978 and 1980 a lot of them discovered Van Halen.

The British music paper *Sounds* (which was later to spawn the current HM bible/comic *Keranng!*) was at the time boosting its circulation by championing new bands; lurching from punk one week to HM the next. It was in their pages that the Van Halen debut album was first reviewed (as an import) in the spring of 1978. Such was the enthusiasm of the reviewer that the piece was headlined "Van Halen, brand new heavy metal heroes". Such was the cynicism of his superiors that underneath the headline, in small print, was the warning "Oh no. Here we go again — Ed". (Historically speaking Van Halen can now sell more seats for one night in Dallas, Texas than *Sounds* can sell copies of their paper in an entire week in the UK.)

"Harsh but refined . . . a hefty punch which also includes breathy subtleties. A magnificent debut. If Van Halen can keep the adrenalin flowing for a second album, then Warners have a winner on their hands."

Prophetic? Warners knew that already. With the States already reacting to the Pasadena Party like it had just been invented (which in a sense it had) it was time to try it out in the good old UK, where it wasn't only the Queen that reigned and a "freeway" was something that told you how heavy you were without you actually having to pay for the privilege.

The heavy metal hardcore audience was the target. The album was released, and with a wonderful sense of uniting the old and the new (the homegrown and the visitors) Van Halen were lined up to play some introductory dates with the venerable Black Sabbath.

It was a good choice. Black Sabbath first emerged from the outskirts of Birmingham in 1968. This was their tenth anniversary outing and the following was hardcore. They were heavy metal incarnate, old wave maybe, but greatly revered. Part of a tradition that Van Halen had absorbed (even if only subliminally) and now, for the sake of the good old pound in the pocket and the start of a quest for worldwide fame they had to take on.

• *Edward the axeman – squeeze me, please me.*

PHOTO: LFI

29

Black Sabbath had roots, and Van Halen had style. As the story goes you'll see that both emerged with a fair amount of credit. But first those roots . . .

Some purists argue that the first real "hard rock" sound came from Liverpool's Big Three, back in 1966. Certainly their drummer was the first to take the back skin off his bass drum for that extra booming sound that has survived to this day. But by 1967 it was groups like the Jimi Hendrix Experience and Cream that were pointing the way; the latter with Eric Clapton strengthening the legend of the guitar hero with virtuoso solos while Ginger Baker double handedly (and double footedly) pushed rock drumming into a new era.

In 1967 Hendrix contributed classics like 'Purple Haze' and 'Hey Joe' to the hard rock catalogue, while in 1968 Cream's 'Wheels Of Fire' was a milestone album. Also in 1968 came Deep Purple with 'Shades Of Deep Purple' — Purple reached their peak with 'Deep Purple In Rock' in 1970 which had all the speed and power that characterised heavy rock. They limped on until 1976 before splitting up to spawn bands like Whitesnake, Rainbow and Gillan. In 1984 — such is the lasting attraction of hard rock — they decided to reform.

In front of a fifty-strong crowd in a North London pub, in 1968, Led Zeppelin made their first public appearance and for many this was the real start. By the time they started touring in earnest (with *Led Zeppelin I* an instant hit on both sides of the Atlantic) they virtually defined a new rock form. The combination of front man Robert Plant with his barechested screaming vocals and the guitar work of Jimmy Page was powerful and enduring. Some say legendary. Christ, Van Halen had grown up on them. Throughout the early seventies (and many argue, beyond) they were a model beyond compare. Instigators and conquerors.

Led Zeppelin, as Van Halen were later to do, transcended labels, but they started something. Jimmy Page noticed the first "headbangers" in Boston in 1970 (eat your heart out Brits!), and while he took Led Zep on to milestones like 'Stairway To Heaven' in 1973 there were plenty of others ready to try and follow on both sides of the Atlantic . . . not to mention places as far apart as Japan and Australia.

The big rush came with the likes of Judas Priest ('British Steel'), UFO, Thin Lizzy and many more in the UK, while Kiss, Montrose, Ted Nugent and Aerosmith were some of the US imports that made cult status (as well as respectable album sales) among the faithful.

Somewhere along the line the whole thing was encapsulated into "heavy metal". A whole mass of rock acts, and an infinitely greater mass of patrons.

Into this maelstrom of volume, technoflash and total devotion to a style of music — of which David Lee Roth later said scathingly: "All came from BB King. It's those same chords. It's just the way you use 'em" — were plunged Van Halen. At Lewisham Odeon to be precise, a smallish theatre in a moderate suburb in South London. Lewisham Odeon has long since closed down, switching to bingo to boost the profits before awaiting the bulldozer. Unlike the Pasadena Civic Auditorium it won't be on the itinerary for Van Halen's farewell tour. A pity really, as it made a little bit of their history. "LEEEEEOOOOOOOOWHISHAAAAM! (Bang! Crash!) YOU ARE THE ROCK AND ROLL CAPITAL OF THE WOOOOORLD!!''

Thus Van Halen first made themselves known to the Great British Public. They put everything into those first opening dates, and even if the sets were short it was obvious to those lucky enough to see them that something new was going on. There hadn't been a figure quite like David Lee Roth on a British stage before ("he thrust himself at the audience with more poses than a Soho stripper" said *Melody Maker*) and Eddie's guitar riffs and showpiece solo was more than enough for the Sabs' fans. They wanted more, and got it.

One fan at Castle Donington in 1984, who remembers seeing Van Halen at the Rainbow (now also closed) on the same tour when he was only sixteen said: "I didn't know much about them, but they were a brilliant support. Really loud and showy. Everything was packed in really tight and we all picked up on 'Runnin' With The Devil' straight away.

"It was a classic really. I got the album as soon as I could afford it."

The groundswell had started; Van Halen, the American upstarts, were in there with the big boys.

Dave 'Monster' Jarrett, who worked for Warners when Van Halen first came over to the UK remembers: "All sorts of rumours started flying around. Heavy metal were two dirty words in those days, after all the punk and New Wave thing, but it was a very solid clique. HM albums were always guaranteed to

• *'Guitar hero Joe Bitch? – I'm just normal'*.

sell a certain amount, and to be honest every major label had one or two, but it was also a case of there being two generations of bands; the old rockers and the upstarts. The young pretenders I suppose.

"When it got around to all the clubs the story was that Van Halen had 'blown the Sabs off stage' and you could sense that things were going to take off."

Van Halen, and particularly David Lee Roth, may not have tuned into the groundswell, but they were certainly prepared to work to establish themselves. Dave loved London. "We had pictures taken everywhere in different costumes, outside Buckingham Palace and the Tower Of London, it was a lot of fun. We did it because we wanted people to know that we'd been to London," he told *Teenage Depression* magazine. "Who wants to see pictures of four guys in jeans and T-shirts leaning up against a wall? So many bands do that.

"When we dressed up and got it together everywhere we went it was like Van Halen day."

Dave, especially bare-chested, was also a natural target. With no signs of age and flab on the one side and his natural gift for loquaciousness on the other he charmed his way through the first round of interviews.

Ros Russell, now a Fleet Street journalist, remem-

PHOTO : RELAY

bers first meeting him. "I didn't interview him as such, it was more a question of seeing if my shorthand could keep up with everything he was saying," she says. "In the end I lost count of the number of times he mentioned Van Halen, but he was genuine. He believed in himself and the band.

"I couldn't help admiring his gall, even if I never did get round to asking him if what was under his Spandex trousers on stage was real."

For Dave Jarrett it was plain sailing. "Dave was the obvious showman and always great value," he says. "The other three weren't as up front but we all got on really well. But always their major priority in England was to work.

"They'd spend hours talking and they'd always have a packed itinerary. They were always really well aware of what needed to be done."

In 1978 Van Halen brushed the singles charts with 'You Really Got Me' and 'Runnin' With The Devil', but the album proved a solid seller, staying in the charts for nearly three months.

In 1979 *Van Halen II* hit the charts in April and Van Halen were back in the UK by the summer — this time as headliners.

The tour was a triumph, but underlying the sell-out nights across the country, there was evidence that Van Halen had changed. With the confidence of platinum success and stadium headlining gigs in the States they'd transcended heavy metal.

The second album was regarded by the hard core in the UK as a "mellowing out" while the band themselves were already calling their sound "Big Rock". Yet it was still the HM diehards who packed out the Odeons.

"Speakers! Lights! Cables! There's more hardware than hall!" said *Sounds* at the time. "Like a dormant volcano the metallic menagerie throbs with barely contained power. It waits to explode." This was in Newcastle; it was, like everywhere Van Halen played "the rock and roll capital of the WORLD!".

As legend has it they only got it wrong once, as

● *The all American Van Halen on stage as the four (below) by two's (right).*

● *David Lee Nuryev in the 'Dance of the Seven Veils'.*

Dave Jarrett recalls: "One night they were playing Coventry, or was it Birmingham? Whatever, the names got mixed up as Dave started his intro and there was more than a bit of confusion.

"But they got away with it, the show was too good for anyone to worry." And nobody did, things were far too loud for that. David carried doing his flying leaps from the drum riser — the splits 12 feet in the air — and lurching around, sublime one minute, ridiculous the next. Alex, hidden away by his enormous kit, thundered away, gathering applause when his drum sticks appeared to catch fire. Michael battered his bass to extinction, throwing it around and jumping on it. Eddie carried on the guitar hero posing, all fast fingers and scorching undertow.

It was everything that rock was, taken to monumental extremes, controlled one minute, a staggering shambles the next, an all-out aural bombardment the minute after. Van Halen had to be seen to be believed. "Believe it, Van Halen music goes BOOM! That's the key to it," said Dave. "It's not folk music you know. Van Halen looks like it sounds, that's the way we live it." And again: "The most extreme type of music will always be the most popular. That's what the people go for, that's what the band and I go for. I love extreme music and I love for it to be presented in an extreme fashion."

Even the *New Musical Express*, at that time the highest selling music paper in Britain (and possibly the most virulently anti-HM) felt obliged to dispatch their star reporter of the day, Nick Kent, to witness "this thing called Van Halen".

Kent, no stranger to excess, came out with horrified comparisons with Led Zeppelin (slightly wide of the mark) and described the concert thus: "The bass and guitar crash in, drums hammer down on a riff so old they were probably playing it on Noah's Ark. Anthony, Van Halen and Roth reel around the stage, flagellating this old riff to death as the latter is doing the splits, teasing his hair, showing off his pectorals, doing hyena like screams and narcissisitically prancing about whilst howling a song which like all other Van Halen songs deals purely with heterosexual lust in a fashion that could all too easily be precised down to one statement of intent, this being 'OK bitch, come here and get down!'"

Later David Lee Roth told Kent: "If you're gonna write a good thing about us then make sure it's real good. But if it's gonna be bad, then make sure it's real bad, a real shitty put down, OK?" It was the latter, or so the *NME* thought, but Dave was already moving into the realms of legend. He had the measure of everybody.

Years later he told one reporter: "I could easily sit here and make you think that all I ever do is party and get drunk. Or I could just as easily make you think, whatever your preconceptions were, that I'm a total health freak." That was true even back in 1979. The "ever quotable David Lee Roth" and his "streams of dialogue on the sex and drugs and rock and roll lifestyle, particularly when they concern Van Halen" were clichés that became legend. Van Halen thrived on it. They'd made their mark — the tour programme boldly stated 'And this is only the beginning . . .' — and what's more they'd made it their own way.

The band went back from the European leg of their world assault with only one niggling doubt. "They couldn't understand how few girls went to the concerts in Europe and Britain," says Dave Jarrett. "They were a bit puzzled at first, but not that it ever caused Dave any problem." The redoubtable Roth even managed to captivate Paula Yates, long time girlfriend of the Boomtown Rats' lead singer Bob Geldof, then a journalist, now a TV presenter. They had an intelligent conversation in Paris and she gave them a good write up. Van Halen were equal to everything.

In 1979 it was "We're gonna be doing some of *Van Halen I* and some of *Van Halen II* and a whole lot of fucking around in between!"

In 1980 they were back with *Women And Children First*, their new album, as their highest new entry. This time it was "We've got brand new music and brand new fuckin' around in between."

They were simply Van Halen, rapidly becoming one of America's biggest exports, if indeed they could actually be persuaded to be exported.

Asked about the New Wave Of British Heavy Metal (which in fact spawned the heavier-than-thou Def Leppard from Sheffield, who went to the States with spotty faces and a lot of hope and ended up snapping at Van Halen's heels in the American albums and singles charts by 1984) there came about the legendary interchange.

David: "And so it came to pass that there was Deep Purple, Led Zeppelin and a host of other bands . . .

PHOTO INSET: LONDON FEATURES INTERNATIONAL

PHOTO: LONDON FEATURES INTERNATIONAL

• *Nose strings attached – the US, the eighties.*

Alex: "And on the seventh day God created Van Halen!"

Meanwhile the musical experts lined up around the block to find out just how Eddie could play the guitar so fast and so well (they usually went away confused but happy) and the journalists turned to tape recorders to catch every last laugh and joke from David Lee Roth.

The moments were worth savouring. Despite the success of the albums and the concerts Blighty was gettng a little expensive. Van Halen didn't yet have anything that amounted to a real hit single, and it was hinted (although firmly denied later) that going from 30,000 seaters in the US of A to 3000 seaters in the UK was getting a little wearisome as well as costing the band and the record company a lot of money.

Maybe, maybe not. As it was Van Halen went back to the States and carried on snowballing. And, apart from a brief racing of the pulses in 1983 when a tour was announced and then cancelled ("They felt that they didn't have any product to promote and that it wasn't worth them coming over," said a Warners spokesman tersely. In fact the on-off tour was the subject of some behind the scenes threats of litigation.) the HM fans and the new converts and those who had just plain missed out weren't to get the chance to see them again until Castle Donington in 1984.

Back then to the land that made them, and was going to make them even bigger.

4. Good evening Colombus (or should that be Cleveland?) — The US 1979–1983

1978 in the US of A was the breakthrough for Van Halen, but while the rest of the world might have witnessed the odd triumph in the years up until 1984 — places as far apart as Lewisham, Japan, Thailand (yes, Thailand) and South America — it was the four solid years of touring from 1979 onwards, across the States and back and back again, that really made the name stick. There were the albums of course; one a year and each outselling the rest. But, truth to tell, it was that "get down, every night's a party night" attitude that took Van Halen to the top — the hard way, though none of them would admit it. Certainly not David Lee Roth, who took to the front night after night, year after year. Pushing himself to extremes on stage while at the same time gradually building up the legend that Van Halen were *the* rock 'n' roll party band of America. People looked for cracks but there didn't seem to be any.

The others just played and played. "We're used to it and it keeps us in shape", Alex once told a surprised interviewer, who'd asked if he ever got fed up, or tired, or both. "It's not a lot different from slogging around California every night, even if the crowds are bigger." And Dave: "Being in Van Halen isn't like being in the Boy Scouts. You don't go home after six weeks with wet pants. You go out and live your music . . ."

By the beginning of 1979 Van Halen were back in the studio with Ted Templeman, cranking out *Van Halen II*, as has been reported, in something under two weeks. Then rehearsals and then the tour.

It was a pattern that was to be repeated. It had to be. Eddie might have produced the off the cuff remark that: "I never expected the first album to happen. I thought we'd make maybe four or five and some people might say 'Oh, yeah! Van Halen, I've heard of them.' Instead we make one album and everybody's heard of us." Eddie, 'Best Newcomer' in *Guitar Player* magazine in 1978, and 'Best Guitarist' in that same magazine for the next five years.

Eddie, the musical driving force behind a potentially all-engulfing mean machine. Yet it was one that had to be worked on, driven hard and driven everywhere before it was accepted.

Quite simply Van Halen, as some people had thought, weren't just invented like the microchip or the Sony Walkman; even if by 1984 they were nearly as popular as both. In reality they were more like door to door salesmen or street vendors with something

● *'Some of those audiences know the words better than I do . . .'*

good to sell. If only you'd look at us! If only you'd come and see us! If only you'd realise what a good time we've got to offer! That's the way it worked in Pasadena. That, eventually was the way it worked across America. There was, it seemed, no other way.

And at least they all believed it. 1980 brought the *Women And Children First* album, 1981 *Fair Warning* and 1982 *Diver Down*, all produced by Ted Templeman, and all notching up a higher rung in the *Billboard* - the US music business Bible - ladder of success.

But behind all this the Van Halen wagon train was forced out on the road. Rock 'n' roll pioneers and buccaneers, fighting for territory and flying the flag.

ALL PHOTOS: LONDON FEATURES INTERNATIONAL

● 'Rock 'n' roll is like Disneyland – there are a million different rides' – David Lee Roth.

Object mission one: plant the seeds, leave behind a string of converts (among the males) and lustful hearts (among the females) across every American state. Object mission two: to put a little bit of Van Halen into everyone under the age of 30. A record, a badge, a T-shirt, or even just a memory.

No band has done it quite that way before in the States (although there are parallels with the way Status Quo hauled themselves to the top in the UK in the seventies, even if they did have hit singles) and, if my prediction is anything to go by, no band will do it quite the same way again. Nor will there ever be quite such a bizarre coupling as David Lee Roth and Edward Van Halen (such a bonding one at that, with no slight at all on the efforts of Michael Anthony and Alex Van Halen). It makes Van Halen unique (if uniquely American), makes you want to like and admire them — even if the eyes and ears aren't always up to the challenge. No wonder David once cited one of his heroes as Ray Kroc, the man who invented McDonald's hamburgers. The other two were Genghis Khan and Alexander the Great. As he told Kristine McKenna (in what was one of the best Van Halen interviews to come out of America): "Kroc did something at a time when everybody told him it couldn't be done.

"Alexander The Great and Genghis Khan ran around the world and consumed it, more for their own benefit than to bring justice or education to people. I think their philosophy was a little bit more legitimate than the 'we're trying to modernise these people' bit, and I have the same philosophy.

"I'm not trying to bring you a message, nor do I want to educate you, but I sure do want to sweep across the world!"

Van Halen had a far harder passage (but a far happier ending so far) than either Alex or Genghis, but bring Big Macs into the picture and the legend fits in a lot more neatly into Roth's and Van Halen's idea of what they were all about. And, damn it, what they did. Put yourself up for consumption anywhere you can and then consume everyone who buys you . . . and have a ball at the same time.

Roth's more oft-quoted quotations fuel the theory. "I just want to make you laugh and make you cry and make you scream and clap . . . and charge ya ten bucks!" In legend Roth always laughs when he says this — that means it's believable.

★ ★ ★ ★

The end (of the show? the party? the tour?) always justified the means. Somewhere in that bombardment between 1979 and 1983 Van Halen created their own version of the eighties white American rock 'n' roll mentality. In a way they'd been born out of the Bi-Centennial but they took the ideals and values of that time right into Ronald Reagan's prime time and messed it up a peach. "We don't go out to work, we go out to play," stated David. And that too became legend. The fantasy world had been previously envisaged, if only briefly, by Sandy Pearlman in his dreams for Blue Oyster Cult way back in 1972, but most of those only made it as far as the album sleeves.

Van Halen were doing it for real. Drinking, smoking, playing; true rock 'n' roll animals. They were even rumoured to have made a film of it (all existence denied, but that's another story). "No-one keeps up with us on the road," said Dave. "Dealers, hangers-on, anybody. After three nights they've had it, flaked. And me, I grab a handful of vitamins and show me to the next gig!"

And for those four years (foreign jaunts excepted) that could have been anywhere. Colombus or Cleveland, even Dave got it wrong sometimes. He fell over plenty of times too, doing the splits in Buffalo (or was it Boston?) but just got up and started all over again. Rumour has it he even went to bed on his own once, in some place like Salina, Kansas.

The rest of the time it was sex and drugs and whatever David wanted you to believe. "Our band has total control over everything we do. We set up our own tours and design everything, our lights, our clothes, our staging. So we've created the ultimate rock 'n' roll dream — our own little fantasy world," he told *Oui* magazine.

And with more than sixty people with fully paid-up parts the play rolled on. "Every day something hurts," Dave once said. "It's that way because you push it. We all attack the whole thing as physically as possible. I drink, I smoke but I also dance, make love and play rock 'n' roll. It's called balancing the string.

"You don't want to be too pure- or too whacked out. But moderation, no!"

The Van Halen tours didn't provide stories as such, no-one was granted that much access. And to date no aide, minder, chaffeur or ex-roadie has chosen to tell the *real* story behind the scenes. Very American that, despite the *National Enquirer* — it's happened to every British rock band from the Stones through Led Zeppelin to Queen. One day, perhaps.

Instead legends and fables grew out of the Van Halen tours. On the surface it was an all-out attack on American convention; a travelling circus that revelled in excess, whether that be in a stack of Marshall amps turned up to full volume (as they always were), or all night drink and drug parties.

Van Halen had hardly been teenagers when Nixon's chosen ones were napalming Vietnam. They weren't too young to remember, just old enough and wise enough to forget. Most of America already had anyway. From 1979 it was Reagan and Uncle Sam against the ageing forces of the Kremlin, and maybe even the massed ranks of the Chinese. The threat of the bomb and instant destruction was in the collective subconscious. Van Halen was a symbolic release.

Reagan smiled and delivered on TV, even when he got shot. Reagan put forward the message that the American way of life would never be challenged, he was the one that was going to press the button if *they* didn't see it our way. Van Halen, simultaneously, had a foot in both camps. If we're going to go let's go with a party(!) — only ten bucks a throw — but let's do it American style. It might have taken four years to prove it but young America saw sense.

Reagan was a movie actor in the forties and fifties, at a time when only the blacks knew how to rock and roll. What price David Lee Roth for President in thirty years time?

For a while they were comfort in crisis, though no critic ever took the time or effort to find out. Excess (however superficial) in the face of repression. Cathartic release when there was nothing else available. Small wonder their tours sold out, and their album sales grew in a geometrical progression that theoretically means that there will be a Van Halen album in every house in the entire United States by 1990 if they carry on.

Van Halen as a band — and whatever role David Lee Roth played as frontman and spokesman — kept their campaign rolling. They gathered the votes, and by 1983 they'd got the nomination. Four subversives on the surface, but underneath a band who were carrying the straightforward values of new young white America to its logical extremes. Van Halen — NOW!!

By 1983 they commanded a fee of one and a half million dollars for one single performance — by a rough estimate what it would cost to fund a Republican convention for an entire week. Reagan versus

● 'Most of what I've learned about music I've learned from Edward and Alex' (below) says David Lee Roth. Most of what he's learned about posing, David taught himself.

PHOTO: RELAY

- LEFT: *'I drink on the job; that's why I got the job!'* – DLR.
- BELOW: *David gets banged to rights in the US of A (and how much did that cost?)*

rock 'n' roll? It wasn't even a contest, as any historian will tell you in twenty years time.

Every undercurrent was there, as reportage reveals. David wasn't "anti-feminist", and all the "racist" jibes were neatly ducked. Van Halen had their "Prom Queens" ("You can't call them groupies any more — the real groupie as they knew it in the seventies is a thing of the past" — Dave). They had their methods of working; according to legend David selected women from the audience with the aid of roadies, via a well worked out walkie talkie routine. "That girl in the fourth row, red T-shirt, get rid of the boyfriend." The roadies did their work . . . and so did Dave. "What do you do when you get a girl

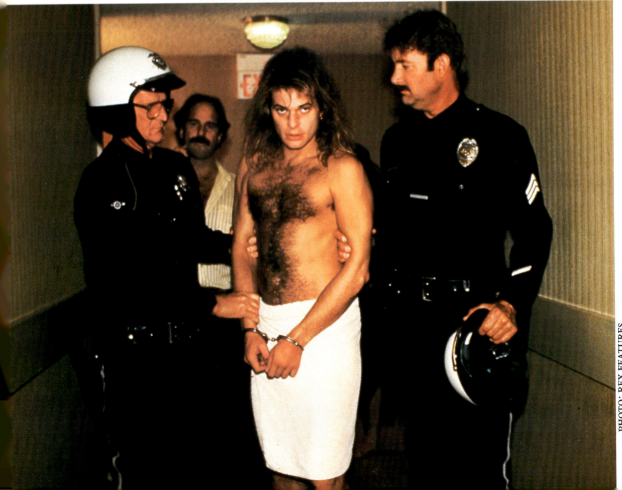

PHOTO: STEVE GRANITZ/LFI

● *'I never fake it – they can always tell from Row 99'* – DLR.

back?" asked *Oui* magazine. "I take off my clothes," Dave replied.

In myth Van Halen worked 300 days a year, performing not only music but every form of excess known to heterosexual, drug-addicted, drink-addicted *man*kind.

In reality it was hard enough. Constant tours, an album to make a year, and just staying alive. Taking rock 'n' roll back to the heartland and keeping it there. Reality states that it only took a third of the alleged time, but the myth was the making . . . and it worked. Van Halen took the reins and held them. The bizarre and unique mixture of David and the Van Halen brothers stuck like glue. It was California, it was rock 'n' roll, it was America in the eighties. ("And we're the soundtrack," added David, much later).

Even the crew, who by 1984 had swelled to around seventy-five paid employees, were a testimony to Van Halen's impeccable sense of time and place. There were a fair number of "Viet vets". Vietnam, almost a generation away from Van Halen, was still present; another part of American culture absorbed into the Van Halen story. Forget, absorb and enjoy. What the Viet vets did and said reportedly surprised David (and maybe still do), even shocked him, but they were in there and part of the legend. The united front.

Most of the facts and myths and legend and everything else about Van Halen in the US up until 1983 is neatly surmised in the apocryphal 'Miscellany' which follows — the Van Halen story that is seen to believed.

Up until the glories of 'Jump' and '1984' (who reads Roman numerals anyway?) there only remains two points to be cleared up. The first is the debunking of the American fable which states that rock stars can survive indefinitely on a diet of cocaine and candy bars. Van Halen didn't, or they wouldn't still be around (and David, for all his press prognostications, shows very little outward signs of wear and tear). Whoever saw him drink more than a Bud for breakfast?

Second (crucially if you believe in American politics and mundanely if you're only interested in the history of a rock band) there were more serious reasons, to the band, for the American onslaught of those four years. It's a fitting end to a finer beginning . . . and if you only want the music turn to Chapter Seven, *without* missing out on Chapter Five!

★ ★ ★ ★

Van Halen toured the states continuously because it was necessary. For the money? Never they said. Indeed David Lee Roth gave plenty of interviewers a hard time over this very subject. Eventually he came up with the stock answer, "If you get into this business for the money you'll have an ulcer in no time." For the prestige? Certainly.

For the sheer pleasure of playing and getting off on rock and roll? That's the story Van Halen wanted everyone to buy — didn't David keep saying "I'm spending ten months a year having a vacation, what could be better than that?" — and eventually buy it they did. Even if it was in the shape of a Van Halen tour jacket for £30. By the end of those four years they had everything organised. Merchandise, adver-

● *Michael Anthony – meat and two potatoes.*

tising, total control. But just put the whole thing in perspective . . . and then move on.

Van Halen slogged it out with punk, New Wave, AOR and even heavy metal imitators for longer than most bands these days take to sell a million singles. All those years in California, and an equal amount of time in Hicksville (as long as the basketball stadium was big enough).

Eddie was happy enough — "this band is like a football team, we all play together," he once said. Alex was happy enough (and even happier when he was dubbed the "practical joker" of the band) and went to lengths to point out that Van Halen weren't heavy metal. "We don't fit into any labels," he once said. "We're Van Halen. But if anything was to describe our sound I reckon the best way to do it would be to call it BIG ROCK. That's the way we see it. That's the way we play it."

Fair enough, big rock it was. And Van Halen pulled out all the stops to make it available.

It was only David, early in the onslaught, who admitted there were a few chinks in the armour. Of the early signing and "overnight success" he once confessed: "We had a manager who ripped us off very carefully and we had to fire him. Then we got the lousiest deal you could imagine, one where we had to sell 1.2 million albums to break even. Break even man! We had no support, nothing." And even as late as 1981, with four platinum albums adorning the family homes of the Roths, Anthonys and Van Halens, David was still able to baldly state: "If this band toured like anybody else this band would be dead. No more Van Halen. "We don't get number one singles, we don't get airplay, we don't get press, we don't get ANYTHING! So all we can do is kick ass ourselves . . ."

Too true. You've heard how they did it. The hard way. It wasn't until early 1983 that Van Halen decided to call their strategic "time out" (for those of you with half an idea about American sport), or as the wonderful Brits would put it, the "half-time change ends!".

1983 was the big one (and wasn't that the time when Ronald Reagan declared that he would stand for another term of office?). Ten years in conception maybe, but that number one single and number one album was just around the corner.

This time the public didn't just pay to come in, they told their friends as well. Enter the second decade of Van Halen . . .

5. Fact and Faction — 1978-1984
A Van Halen Miscellany

"If but one word be true . . ." said some old Limey playwright back in the mists of time (Ben Jonson, I think it was).

And here, for history's sake, are some of them to do with the story of Van Halen. They're a band who've made records and broken records and done more than a few other things along the way.

This miscellany isn't 'Van Halen — This Is Your Life'; far from it. Rather it's a collection of achievements, quotable quotations, worthy triumphs and sheer and utter nonsense.

More to the point it's the way Van Halen have been looked at, are looked at, and how they look at themselves in that public arena of rock 'n' roll they chose to make their lives. And, indeed, their legend.

"Sex and drugs and rock 'n' roll, when I say it, when they hear it and respond to it, it is not a literal translation. It's a whole lot more. That is merely a stereotype for the whole attitude, the way of behaving, and way of living your life, and approaching the various obstacles in your life. The rent, the wife, the girlfriend, the teacher, the probation officer. So you say 'sex, drugs and rock 'n' roll'."

David Lee Roth talking to a fan in 1981

"I'm not showing off anything — it's just the most euphoric feeling. It's better, no, not better, but it's like coming. It's like sex, except different."

Edward Van Halen

● *From this (below) to this (right) in one easy lesson – a tribute to the power of M & M's . . . and certainly not the brown ones.*

● *Edward The First – definitely not a Jungle Stud.*

"See that number on my guitar? 5150. It's the Los Angeles police code for an escaped mental case. Actually, in the band, I'm considered the freak."

Edward Van Halen

David Lee Roth took out an insurance policy with Lloyd's of London against paternity suits in 1980. The policy covers up to £50,000 in legal costs for one year with £2000 deductible to eliminate nuisance claims. Roth claimed he convinced Lloyd's that debauchery was 'instrumental' to his work.

"It's really difficult to deal with the hordes of eighteen to twenty-five year old women in sexy clothes who swamp you outside the hotel."

"We're not heavy metal. I'm a *musician*."

Edward Van Halen

Interviewer: "What do you set your volume and tone on?"
Edward Van Halen: "Everything on ten, that's it."

Sounds: "Do you ever get turned down by women?"
David Lee Roth: "I never ask."

The only Van Halen single to sell more than a million copies worldwide is 'Jump'. Midway through 1984 it was estimated to have sold over 2.5 million worldwide, including well over a million in America, where it stayed at number one for five weeks.

"I guess I can see the influence I've had. Every time I put the radio on nowadays I hear a lot of me. Sometimes it pisses me off, sometimes it makes me feel good. I just don't think about it."

Edward Van Halen in 1983

"If you really want to send a message I always say — use Western Union. We're just about love songs, man!"

David Lee Roth

"I feel like a shining example, but I'm not sure of what."

David Lee Roth

The runaway success of 'Jump' forced the Pointer Sisters to re-name their album track of the same name 'Jump (For My Love)' when they released it as a single.

"Everything you read is true. I live and breathe and do four times as much four times as fast as anyone else. Someone titled an album *Babylon By Bus*, well, that describes us perfectly."

David Lee Roth

"Our parents always wanted us to become concert pianists. They got real uptight when we started to rock."

Edward Van Halen

"Everything I do on stage is transmuted from other things. *The Ed Sullivan Show*, for instance. You see some Russian dancers and you go, 'Hey, I can do that. I'm gonna change it, and I'm gonna do it this way, and I'm gonna wait and do it like that. An nobody's going to recognise it by then anyway, so it's mine.' That is the beauty of rock and roll. There must be no rules and no schools. You just make it up as you go."

David Lee Roth

The ultimate accolade? Sixties eccentric Tiny Tim, who carries his belongings around in a plastic bag, sings in a thin vibrato and married his first wife on TV, enthused over Van Halen: "They're my favourite band in the whole world — except for Herb Alpert & The Tijuana Brass."

"This band is the distillation of every vulgar trend that has surfaced in over twenty years of rock 'n' roll history."

Good Times

"It's about what everybody feels on a Friday or Saturday night. You come home from work or school, you have your bath, you shave, you jump in your car, you pick up your girlfriend and you're gonna have a good time. Well, with Van Halen, *every* night's a Saturday night."

Michael Anthony

"The idea is not the pot of gold, but the rainbow itself."

David Lee Roth

In contrast to their limited success as a singles band, all six of Van Halen's albums have gone platinum (one million sales) in America — and each album has outsold its predecessors.

"It's the glamour, the tinsel, the non-stop, late-night endless party that is the crest of the biggest wave with spray in your face. It's the laugh in the face of death blown out of proportion — mutated reality that is the

BOTH PHOTOS: LONDON FEATURES INTERNATIONAL

● *On stage, in tune, Van Halen live in the eighties. 'It is theatrical', says David Lee Roth. 'You're charging money, you don't have an off night'.*

wonderful, wacky, crazy, cut-up, cutey world of rock 'n' roll!"

David Lee Roth

"If I weren't playing in an arena, if I were playing a club, I'd still be doing it because that's what I want to do. I love playing the guitar."

Edward Van Halen

"I'm not here to be an artist. You can make *some* art out of it, but how artistic can you be in a place where they sell popcorn?"

David Lee Roth

The largest fee ever paid for a rock band to perform is $1,500,000 paid to Van Halen for their set at the 'US '83 Festival' in San Bernadino on May 29, 1983. They payment was equalled the following day by the fee paid to headlining David Bowie. The festival was not a success, attracting only 300,000 people, when up to 750,000 had been expected. Financier Steve Wozniak eventually returned a loss of nearly ten million dollars on the event.

"We don't get out there and pretend we're 'artists'. We are out there to have a good time and to enjoy it with 10,000 of our closest friends, or however large the hall is."

Alex Van Halen

"A band has emerged from out of the land of celluloid heroes and ever-present sunshine that threatens to

PHOTO: REX FEATURES

literally blast apart all of our notions concerning the 'laid back' music of California.''

New York Daily News

"Van Halen is entertainment. Van Halen is entertainment delivered at maximum impact, but it's entertainment."

David Lee Roth

Eddie Van Halen is married to American soap opera actress Valerie Bertinelli, who made her name in the *One Day At A Time* series. Michael Anthony is also married.

"One of the most ill-bred, under-skilled, over-amplified noise machines ever to make it big in rock, Van Halen showed a screaming Civic Centre audience just how low entertainment can sink."

Hartford Courant

"Here is rock and roll the way it should be played. Van Halen will be around for a long time after many so-called superstars have gone into oblivion. This band is excellent all the way around."

Providence Journal

"A lot of bands wait for the audience to give a spark. I go onstage with a flamethrower."

David Lee Roth

Van Halen's second world tour, in 1979, was one of the longest ever completed by a rock band. It rumbled on for ten months. Spare a thought for the roadies, who were away from home for the whole time, and had to maintain and shift 22 tons of sound equipment and ten tons of lights.

"Hey, there's no two ways about it, Van Halen is as obnoxious as it gets."

Creem magazine

"Tell him not to ask any stupid questions."

Alex Van Halen as overheard by an interviewer

"I respect the press because they have good vocabularies, and they know how to use adjectives to say what they feel, but besides that, they are just another set of bozos listening to the radio just like you and me and everbody else. If you are a critic, chances are you have a better vocabulary to use in describing why you don't like something. So I respect them."

David Lee Roth

October 22, 1982 was declared Van Halen day in Worcester, Massachusetts.

"David Lee Roth is Van Halen's spokesman, an extra-curricular task he takes to like fish to water. A more overt exhibitionist it would be right impossible to locate, either in rock 'n' roll or used car salesmanship."

New Musical Express

"Van Halen is the latest rock act to fall out of a family tree of deadbeats whose ancestry includes slave drummers of Roman galleys, Ginger Baker's Air Force and the street crews of the New York City Department of Sanitation."

Rolling Stone

British and American royalty organisations have logged over twenty covers of 'Jump', including versions by the Freeform Wind Ensemble (!), James Last (unreleased as yet), Gadfly (a ten minute disco re-interpretation) and Scotland's Aztec Camera who tackled the song on the flip of their 'All I Need Is Everything' single, imbuing it with a fine, understated guitar treatment.

"Originally I played drums and my brother played guitar. While I was out throwing papers he was practising my drums. He did it better than I did and I said, 'Okay, you play my drums, I'll pick your guitar' and it went from there."

Edward Van Halen

"How long have you guys been together?"

Question posed to the brothers Van Halen by an American radio DJ

After Van Halen made Roy Orbison's 'Oh Pretty Woman' an American Top Twenty hit in 1982, the Big O was said to be impressed and actively considering reciprocating by recording his own version of a Van Halen song. Apparently he didn't find one suitable.

"If you get into this for the money, you'll have an ulcer in no time. You won't have a hit just when you need it and you'll break up with your girl and even your dog won't recognise you. The idea at heart is — how much do you like to play? I like it a whole lot and so does the band. That doesn't mean just up on stage."

David Lee Roth

"I honestly feel that audience participation extends from onstage to backstage to under the stage."

David Lee Roth

Eddie Van Halen achieved a rare distinction in 1984, when two consecutive singles releases bearing his fretwork reached the top of the American charts. First, Michael Jackson topped the charts with 'Beat It', on which Eddie guested, and a couple of months later Van Halen's own 'Jump' reached the top. Eddie also played guitar on Brian May's Starfleet album, but no single was pulled from the album in America.

"Van Halen is an animated 'Heavy Metal' comic book and these guys are living it."

Steve Vando, road manager

• *Eddie and Valerie: 'We're just two ordinary schmoes who got married'.*

"When I was eight or nine, they said I was hyperactive. After dinner, when I got the blood sugar level up, I would be drumming with my silverware or singing television commercials. My parents would tell the company, 'Oh don't worry, David's just doing what we call Monkey Hour'. Well, I turned Monkey Hour into a career."

David Lee Roth

'Dance The Night Away' was released as a limited (5000) edition picture disc in the UK.

"I play for self-satisfaction, but it makes it even better when other people enjoy it."

Edward Van Halen

PHOTO: REX FEATURES

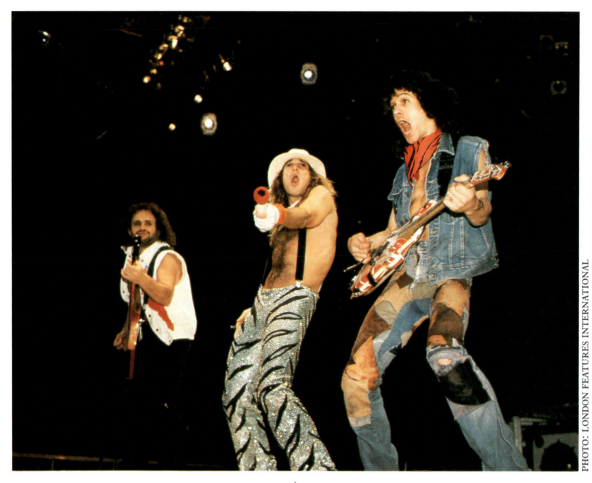

PHOTO: LONDON FEATURES INTERNATIONAL

"Eddie is one of the hottest and most uninhibited young guitarists around."

Guitar Player magazine

Van Halen have twice raided the Ray Davies songbook, recording 'Where Have All The Good Times Gone' and 'You Really Got Me'. Only Larry Page and James Last (that man again!) have recorded more of Davies's songs — apart, of course, from the Kinks.

"I went and played with Alex and Ed for three hours in a little garage they were rehearsing in. They tried to put me through every beat change and off-beat thing they could think of, and I caught them all! Right after we were through playing they just said 'You want to join the band?' I said, 'Sure!'"

Michael Anthony

"Roth is very beautiful, cocky and shameless, and the strut is his natural gait. Affecting delicious perversity, he is really an over-petted child with a swell sense of humour and a superb ass."

Oui magazine

Via his guest appearance on 'Beat It', Eddie Van Halen is one of the elite band of musicians who can claim to have played on the world's best-selling album — Michael Jackson's 'Thriller', most recently estimated as having sold forty million copies.

● *'You sing and I'll sing; you point and I'll point . . .'*

"I play the instrument I have."

David Lee Roth

"And what an instrument!"

US magazine

A British band the Cockney Rejects lauded Van Halen with their own tribute in 1980 — with a song called 'Van Bollocks'.

"That's My Boy!"

David Lee Roth's grandmother

"Van Halen touches a responsive chord. It's sort of a deliverance. Some people go to church for that feeling. Some go to hockey games. The rest of 'em come to Van Halen."

David Lee Roth

Apart from videos and TV specials Van Halen have yet to appear in front of the movie cameras. But rumour and legend still surrounds the making of the infamous Van Halen behind-the-scenes "porn" movie. It was reported that the group had hired a Dutch cameraman to film some hotel room action but this was never seen. David Lee Roth told *Oui* magazine in America later:

58

"Until we really are offered a vehicle that fits Van Halen I'd prefer to star in a driver education movie, instead of just taking my clothes off in a fuck flick."

However Roth also spilled the beans on one video that *was* made and, with apologies and grateful thanks to *Oui*, this was the story:

"It was somewhere around Detroit and I'd just come back to the hotel from some scene. I'm walking down the hall — we usually rent out an entire floor — and I hear a lot of noise. There's a door open and inside about twenty people, cheering and clapping. I walk in and I see there's one girl, just one, and she's doing up every single guy. In every way imagin-

● *'OK Paul, you can turn the wind machine off now'*.

able. Somebody's got our video camera that we always travel with and he's recording the whole thing for posterity. I went and got my stereo and played the theme tune from *Jaws* while everything possible sexually was going on." It was an all-night party, one which Roth said that the hotel charged over a thousand dollars to clear up afterwards, but again the footage shot has never been seen outside the Van Halen camp. To complete the apocryphal tale Roth told *Oui*: "The upshot is that the girl ended up marrying one of the guys in the crew, and they've lived happily ever after."

"If Van Halen ever fails, Roth can aways head for Las Vegas, where a second career awaits him. Take this singer, please."

Washington Post

"The band you love to hate."

Soho News

Following a concert at Cincinnati's Riverfront Coliseum in 1980, David Lee Roth was accused of inciting the crowd to smoke during his performance, in violation of an Ohio law that makes illegal 'soliciting, aiding or abetting another in committing an offence, to wit: smoking." He was freed on a $5000 bond. All charges were later dropped, although David considered a civil suit for violation of civil rights.

"You gotta keep in mind you don't go *work* music, you *play* music. You don't go on the road to work. You go on the road to play. I think that's real important."

David Lee Roth

"I want to write for your magazine. I hate David Lee Roth. Do I qualify?"

Letter to *Creem* magazine
(The Editor replied: "You and many of our readers")

Van Halen is the only act to name an American hit after the South American state of Panama — but nine other countries have been named in US Top Forty hits. Bob Moore hit with 'Mexico', Harry Belafonte with 'Jamaica Farewell' and Roger Miller with 'England Swings'. Dick Jacobs scored with 'Petticoat Of Portugal', George Harrison with 'Bangla Desh' and the Ritchie Family with 'Brazil'. Finally, Paul McCartney demanded 'Give Ireland Back To The Irish', Three Dog Night admitted they'd 'Never Been To Spain' and David Bowie sang the praises of his 'China Girl'.

"We're not this way because we're in a rock 'n' roll band — we're in a rock 'n' roll band because we are this way."

Michael Anthony

"I get a kick out of these people who sing about, 'Oh, we're gonna do it all night, and then we're going to get in the backseat of the car and do it again, then I'm going to drink like crazy, and turn it up too loud and we're gonna crash the car' and then the musicians walk to the side of the stage and there's the wife, three kids, the station wagon with the fake wood on the side

parked by the door, and there's an incongruity there, it doesn't quite match up."

David Lee Roth

Photographer Helmut Newton, more used to Vogue than Van Halen, entered the legend briefly when he shot the picture that appeared as a poster inside the *Women And Children First* album in 1980. It showed a bare-chested Roth chained to a wire fence by his hands and stirred up a small ripple of controversy for "encouraging bondage", although the story was more of a down page paragraph than prime time TV material. "It was just one of those things we did," Roth was reported to have said. "He was in town and we were in town and it happened." According to unverified reports Newton was paid $40.

"Hey I'm just a kid just as much as the kids who come to see us. Not long ago I was out there, watching other bands."

Edward Van Halen

"I don't ever want Van Halen on the same bill as me!"

Ted Nugent

A clause in Van Halen's contract stipulates that no brown Smarties (M&M's in the USA) should be provided as part of their backstage provisions. This led to the much publicised "food riot" in New Mexico, when the brown ones were inadvertently left in, and the band proceeded to throw the rest of the food around. The incident led to a few 'Van Halen are racist' jibes, but was quickly forgotten. David Lee Roth sideswiped the incident in a later interview by saying: "Everything we do is in our own control, right down to the M&M's backstage."

"When you drive, you follow the hood ornament. The rear view mirror is only good for seeing how good you look while you're getting there."

David Lee Roth

David Lee Roth: "There's a little Van Halen in all of us."

New Musical Express: "Is there a Catholic Priest in the house?"

In 1984 WEA were fined £6000 for the alleged 'hyping' of the 'Jump' single in the UK. This provoked the following response from Rob Dickins, WEA UK Chairman, in response to the BPI fine:

"Jump, by Van Halen, was a No. 1 in the USA and has been a top ten hit around the rest of the world.

PHOTO: PICTORIAL PRESS

The success in the UK confirms the quality of this single. I would like to point out that the offence was the result of over-enthusiasm for a great record by a few salesmen and not company policy. I would also like to stress that the product concerned was of the same artist. In no way was one artist's product used to promote another."

"A song is a song is a song. For example, 'You Really Got Me' goes back to the bar days. We used to play it then, we still play it now, and everybody likes it. We like it, the audiences likes it, and everybody's happy. Even Ray Davies."

Alex Van Halen

Van Halen hit problems in British stores over their 'offensive and inappropriate' record sleeves in 1984. The covers of both the single 'Jump' and the album '1984', depict an angelic baby with wings smoking a cigarette. And WH Smith shops refused to put the records on sale until the sleeves were changed.

WEA Records, on behalf of Warner Brothers, then supplied the chain store with singles in plain bags and albums with stickers covering the controversial part of the sleeve.

"If the song is right and fits our style, and if we can arrange it to fit our style, then we'll do it."

Michael Anthony

'House Of Pain', which finally appeared as a track on the '1984' album, first surfaced as a Van Halen song back in 1976 as one of the tracks on the demo tape funded by Gene Simmons of Kiss.

"Van Halen will never be confused with Johnny Mathis."

Twin Cities Reader

Mormons in Salt Lake City reportedly recommended that Van Halen's '1984' should not be sold within the city limits because of its sleeve's depiction of a cherub smoking. Elsewhere, 'Jump' was criticised for encouraging suicide . . .

"Success is something you give yourself, fame is what other people give you."

David Lee Roth

When *Time*, the flashy news magazine, decreed that Ronald Regan and Andropov (RIP) would jointly share its MAN OF THE YEAR award, a Brazilian gentleman wrote in to disagree. David Lee Roth, 'lead singer with the rock band Van Halen', should get it he reckoned, a man who 'in a time of crisis and world tension brings joy to the hearts of millions of young people'.

"A lot of people take Van Halen more seriously than we do."

David Lee Roth

"Van Halen, it's the real thing baby."
David Lee Roth to a reporter on his first British tour in 1978

David Lee Roth belongs to an organisation called The Jungle Studs. As he told *Kerrangg!*'s Laura Canyon early in 1984:
"It's been going for around four years now, and it sort of hails back to the Jack London, White Fang Of The North, Tarzan swinging through the trees sort of fantasies. There's I guess, fourteen of us now, and I'm the only one in music. The other fellows are all computer programmers or dope dealers, you name it!"
The Jungle Studs were airlifted into the Amazon rain forest for six weeks a while back, and the plan for October 1984, the month of Dave's birthday, was for a foray into Papua, New Guinea with only themselves and rucksacks for company. (Ted Nugent, it is reliably reported, is *not* a member of the Jungle Studs!).

"People walk out of our shows three feet off the ground. It's like a car could hit you and nothing would happen."

David Lee Roth

"Don't stick your tongue out at me unless you intend to use it."
David Lee Roth to the audience at Donington, 1984.

"I saw who threw that bottle and I'm going to fuck your girlfriend."

David Lee Roth to the same audience

Eddie Van Halen reportedly strengthens his fingers by climbing up the backyard wall at his home studio, once said he boiled his guitar strings before using them on stage, and has been known to stay up for three days and three nights playing guitar. He was also once at a party where Eric Clapton was also in attendance but later said:
"I got drunk and kind of blew it. There he was and all I could do was go 'Hi!' and sort of walk away."

"I'm a real family-orientated guy. In fact I've started three or four since January."
David Lee Roth, joking for the benefit of the
Daily Mirror before Donington in 1984

"I used to have a drug problem, now I can afford it."
David Lee Roth, as above

"I can get much better pictures of him when he's got make-up on."
A Japanese photographer backstage at Donington, 1984

6. Off and on — the music 1978–1984

ON...

Van Halen came into their own on stage, and since their first real funding (after the deal in 1978) they've spared no time or expense into turning their "show" (for it's actually a lot more than that) into a Van Halen "experience".

It's the logical extension of the "every night's a Saturday night" theory. Trucked across the States, flown across the world, here today, gone tomorrow. And, they claim, you always get your money's worth — Houston, Buffalo, Lewisham, Donington, the message is, this is for you!

In Britain everybody who saw them between 1978 and 1980 were, in a word, *shocked*, by the sheer size and scale of the Starship Halen wherever and whenever it docked.

By 1984, by the law of geometrical progression dictated by the success of their album sales, things were even bigger, even louder, even more spectacular. Possibly the most expensive rock 'n' roll extravaganza ever mounted (that was before the Jacksons, although it's not really the same thing!). 120 tons of equipment, a crew of over seventy; all there to squeeze out energy, technoflash and rock 'n' roll extremity to its absolute limit. Who cares about the money, we're putting on a SHOW! The message came over loud and clear.

To one American fan, the aforementioned Gillian Bigelou (how are ya out there in Santa Barbara these days?), Van Halen "took over where everyone else left off, and they're still there. They don't need raw meat on stage, they don't need to play around with chainsaws, like all the LA HM also rans are trying to do. They *are* raw meat, and they do a lot more damage than a toy chainsaw."

The more churlish, especially the English critics, put Van Halen into the realms of "the ultimate rock 'n' roll parody, but also the ultimate rock 'n' roll experience." Fortunately most people didn't see it that way. Gillian: "It's not a case of watching or listening, you want to get off on the whole thing. OK, so you get Dave spouting out a load of garbage sometimes, and forgetting the words, and all the songs collapse in the middle, and it's an unholy mess of sound and lights but Van Halen never leave you halfway there.

"They kind of take you over, and it's worth it in the end."

● *Alex in one of his more flattering poses (© Simon Tebbutt).*

The show has *evolved* of course, over the years; new numbers added, more lights (in the last incarnation the whole back rig turned a complete circle behind the drum riser to reveal the Roman numerals of 1984 — yee hi!!) but it has always been essentially the same. In short a gloriously choreographed shambles, held together by spirit and volume. Always seemingly out of control, always just holding on to it. Delightful. The comparisons between other forms of spiritual, sexual and narcotic pleasure are endless . . . and Van Halen mean it to be that way. "We practise 'screaming sports'," David once said. "You know when you get to your limit and start to get out of control try screaming! sometimes it pulls you through, and what an experience . . ."

Van Halen are also theatre and entertainment, in great big illuminated capital letters. "It's showbiz, and there's a lot to be said for consistent play. Like the theatre," says Dave. "When you're charging good money you don't have an off night."

PHOTO: LFI

• *'And I thought some jerk was going to turn the water on . . .'*

And, to be honest, they don't have many different ones either. Everywhere is "THE ROCK AND ROLL CAPITAL OF THE WORLD!" (just like Lewisham). Dave, more often than not, will prance on in the style of the day (hell, look at the pictures!) and scream "I hear the guy who invented rock 'n' roll came from (insert name of town)" CRASH! "I hear that the guy who invented sex and drugs also came from (insert name of town)" CRASH! In legend this is greeted with roars of approval . . . the start of the show.

Then it's two hours of strutting and posing and jumping (and in 1984 a Kung Fu — pek kwar — dance with real swords) led by Ringmaster Roth. "It's like maybe 110 degrees out there under the lights, and you flex yourself, and hold a note and scream till it feels like you're going to pass out. Then you're ready for the next song."

Alex thunders away behind his kit (usually no less than two complete sets), Eddie gets his gut-wrenching, vein-popping solos, and Michael Anthony ("he's rock solid, it makes up for Eddie and I being too energetic at times," says Dave) bruising and abusing his Jack Daniels bottle bass guitar, even to the extent of throwing it around or jumping onto it from a speaker stack.

Devastating. Never exactly a musical treat, and how real is that on stage party anyway? But for any true student of big rock excess Van Halen have made themselves (at whatever cost) into one band that's got to be seen at least once — and, whatever you read about anyone else, that is one truly magnificent achievement.

"The drum riser is say about six feet, and I get maybe six feet in the air," David always used to say about his 'flying splits' (he tapes his legs before the show for protection, but that's never been brought to the attention of the Arts Council). "So I'm coming in from maybe 12 feet in the air. Going up is no problem. Coming down is the whole ball of wax . . ." Which, naturally enough, leads to the albums . . .

. . . OFF

David doesn't do the splits in the studio, but the entirely believable legend is that he does virtually

● ABOVE: *Man at C & A meets . . . the man from the ICA*: RIGHT

PHOTO: PAUL CANTY/LFI

"We all play together and if it needs a rhythm track I'll overdub it instead of the other way round. It goes so much quicker that way. If you listen ninety per cent of the album is live. It only took ten days to record the second album. And the vocals are all done at the same time, even if it's only for a guide. They're done again if you get guitar noise going into the vocal tracks."

Of course things changed, but not a lot. By the fourth album, *Fair Warning*, the "live" atmosphere was still there, but with drums and lead guitar right up front, the bass right back, and David (even by his own admission not the world's greatest singer) shouting and singing somewhere in between.

As for artistic merit? In America the albums were greeted as a logical sequence ("OK, so Van Halen have basically been making the same album since their atomic-bop debut in 1978, but what's wrong with a drop of their joy-juice once a year?" were the entirely laudable sentiments of David Fricke). In Britain they were rationalised, and in some cases dismissed out of hand. Other more loyal followers revelled in what *Sounds* called "the extremes of shambling chaos".

But what emerged before 'Jump' and '1984' was what Van Halen had had you believe all along. Their albums were an "experience", born of the stage and the show and whatever they got up to in between. Songs didn't leap out at you, rather the album bludgeoned you into submission if you played it loud enough, got drunk enough, or didn't think too much. That, they were saying, was the very antithesis of the Van Halen ethic. Indeed there was scarcely a song to remember, but the sound? Now that was unmistakeably Van Halen. Even case-hardened musos could tell without even a sideways glance at the sleeve.

The music was credited to Van Halen. Alex and Michael did come up with a workable riff or two, but it was Eddie who really laid it down. David, meanwhile, searched here, there and everywhere and came up with the lyrics. "I like all kinds of music and I steal from everybody. You have to steal it from somebody and learn it just the way it is," he said. "Then you change the beginning and you change the end and by that time you've got an even better idea for the middle. By the time you put it on plastic nobody recognises it. In fact you don't recognise it yourself after the eighth time you've sung it. "*That's* where the inspiration comes from!"

everything else he does on stage. As do the rest of the band. "The albums come out of what we do on stage" is one of the oldest Van Halen clichés around. Well worn, well documented, and given a pinch of salt, not entirely removed from the truth.

Ted Templeman has been there from the beginning as producer, with engineer Donn Landee (working closely in conjunction with Edward on mixing) a latterly important figure.

'*Van Halen*', the first album, set the pattern that was to be repeated. Quite simply play live in the studio, and something will come out. Ted believed, and got the results.

As Edward told *International Musician* after *Van Halen II*: "What they do with most bands is lay down a rhythm track and then add on a solo. I can't stand doing that so what I do is solo on the basic track because I like playing with people. I'm not into playing with machines."

The two extremes were Eddie, doodling on the guitar, and David, claiming as he did that he wrote his lyrics any time, anywhere that suited him. The result, the fusion, was something that sounded like an indistinguishable grinding of HM garbage from behind a typewriter but quite different in front of a turntable or a grotesquely illuminated stage. That's when it gets to you.

Whether the music made the myth or the myth made the music is still a matter of conjecture . . . and will likely remain one. Van Halen seem likely to continue on the same roller coaster path. "We haven't matured musically, we haven't started sending out messages," David said recently. "We're still doing the same things."

'1984', with the benefit of the year's breathing space, was a welcome shock, for diehards and cynics alike. Similarly 'Jump' and 'I'll Wait' with the synths were a "change" worthy of note (the success of the singles even more worthy). Yet until the band implodes or the world explodes Van Halen will continue as before; there's reputedly a large stock of material that didn't get used for '1984'.

Sure Van Halen would love another really big hit single (wouldn't we all?) but until it comes hold on to the six cards that have already been dealt. If you're sweating, it's a safe bet that the new album won't be called either *Van Halen 7*, *Van Halen Live* or *1985*. Confident in their music, yes. Perverse in its presentation . . . never!

7 Jump! — The world 1983–1984

"I get up . . . and nothing gets me down"
(from 'Jump', 1984)

1983 was the start of a second decade for Van Halen. The whole year was remarkable for its lack of vinyl but at the end of the day it affected the band's status not a whit. It was a time when the batteries were recharged. The non-stop tour/album pattern rescinded for the first time since 1978; and air was cleared. In a way Van Halen had proved their point. They were standing back and taking stock, even if this was never actually stated at the time. Call it luck, call it circumstance; without that "break" they would never have leaped back into legend in 1984. And it wasn't only Van Halen who were taking a long hard look. So was Joe and Jane Public in the States (but just make that Joe Public for the UK for the time being), so were their maligners — and *not* only the rock critics — so too were the mighty Warners.

● *Michael: not all the beef from Chicago goes East.*

The chronology was pretty straightforward, but for the first time since, say 1973, the story wasn't a fast-forward, full volume blur, punctuated at odd intervals by guitar solos from Eddie or ever-enlargeable quotes from David Lee Roth. That was *already* legend. Somehow Van Halen needed something new and it was the rumours, the random events, and the whole lazy, crazy year of 1983 that provided it.

In 1982 *Diver Down* peaked at number three in the Billboard chart, up until then their highest position. Musically speaking it was a low, however. More covers than classics, it sold in the States on the back of a hefty tour, but only brushed the UK charts for just over a month, tottering up to thirty-six before disappearing amidst a pretty severe pasting from the hard core British HM hacks.

Yet 1983 started with a planned tour of the UK, cancelled at the record company's insistence, and a few dates in South America. Van Halen were back in March to start work on the new album. In the end up it took "about a year, and then we were a week late,"

● *Face to face . . .*
. . . modern America's deadliest duo.

PHOTO: LFI

David later joked. Eddie was much more laconic. "I'd say it probably took about a month to actually record and mix, but what with everything else going on that month was probably spread out over the whole year. It seemed to take a long time, to us it did anyway," he told *International Musician*. Not that the lack of product was really a problem. Van Halen were . . . Van Halen. Firmly embedded in the American consciousness. All those albums and T-shirts and badges were proudly displayed in homes around the heartland.

The group might have bemoaned the lack of support, the lack of hit singles, the lack of media attention, but somehow they'd surpassed it all.

Even before '1984' was recorded producer Ted Templeman had been quoted as saying that Eddie was "the greatest guitarist alive", while other commentators were prone to saying things like "he has spawned more imitators than Clapton, and created more technical mysteries than Hendrix at his best" and other reams of superlatives. David, meanwhile, was the "blond Dionysus", a proud strutting rock 'n' roll animal, imitated in everything from his clothes sense to his movements on stage and off. Imitated indeed, right down to his "interview technique". And, lest we not forget Alex and Michael Anthony, they were "the rhythm section that every rock band would give their advance for".

Two parallel, but vastly different, legends and two entirely indispensable sidekicks. Why, godamnit, did they stay together? Quite simply because nobody asked them until a year later and by then the crisis — what crisis? — was over. Even the fearless Brits, with the headbangers' hopes raised sky high by the prospect of seeing VH in the flesh for the first time in three years, kept strangely quiet. No tour, no album? No comment.

Van Halen, meanwhile, went about their merry way — and, according to legend, argued the whole time. After all friction fuels the fire and as David was later to say (wise after the event perhaps, but still light years ahead of everybody else): "This is 1984 and we're going all out for it — uncontrollable arson. Who wants to play with matches when you can use a pipe bomb?"

In reality three things happened in 1983 that brought the Van Halen myth out into the open. Separate, but intertwined, they were like three tracks put down on a mixing console, and by January 1984

bonded together so tightly, so uniquely that the end result was spectacular. It was meant to be that way.

Track one: Van Halen commanded the highest fee for a rock group for one performance at the US Festival in California; a cool million and a half dollars.

Track two: Eddie Van Halen lent his services to Michael Jackson and Quincy Jones when they recorded 'Beat It', a chart topping single from the chart topping *Thriller* album.

Track three: Somewhere along the way Eddie's music incorporated synths, and by the autumn David had accepted it and wrote the lyrics for all the tracks.

With impeccable timing, if not exactly brilliantly original titling, the '1984' album (along with its neat little baby, the single 'Jump') was released in January 1984. Symbiosis? Chemistry? Luck?

As it goes, a bit of all three.

The strategic stop worked a treat, and all the stories came out afterwards. It wouldn't be legend otherwise.

The US Festival was a landmark, and if it was a financial disaster for the promoter at least it got Van Halen into the Guinness Book Of Records (look under "highest paid group"). David was reticent at the time, certainly off stage (on stage he created more than a few ripples by slagging off the Clash) although he later professed to "really enjoying it. It was our own backyard, just like Anaheim all over again, and I think we went down really well. It was good to play in front of that many people."

At 300,000 a mere hundred times the amount that had packed the Pasadena Civic all those years ago. David Bowie played the next day for the same fee, but all the media coverage, the TV and general brouhaha, kept Van Halen bubbling. In the savage land of American groupdom they were still the top dogs. Some might have bet on a live album but it was never really on the cards, and never has been ("We don't need to," they've all said at one time or another). 'Twas merely a milestone.

Eddie later expressed frustration about the whole shebang. As a showman Dave might have got off on it, but it was another gig, it got in the way of the music. The US Festival screwed everything up," he told *International Musician* months later. "It was like the shortest tour in the world. The preparations for that one gig was like doing a whole tour. We had to rent a sound stage and set up and rehearse again

• *'Anything my brother can look, I can look worse'*.

because we hadn't played in front of people for so long.

"Then there was the video; there were all kinds of problems with cameramen not getting good shots of the band and not focusing on the band members when we were doing solos. I tell you, the whole thing was a nightmare. It kept haunting us, and we had a TV to deliver to them too. So, all these things kept popping up and we were going 'Goddam, is this US thing ever going to be over?'"

It was, and it's still being talked about a year later — a bit like the "parachute jump" really, but this was strictly kosher. As David said: "Van Halen have broken just about every record there is in terms of crowds, tours, T-shirts, everything. What's another record?"

Despite the pressure to record the album, and the hassles of US Festival, there was a tacit understanding that Van Halen were loosening up a little, taking the opportunity "to go their own ways". Dave managed to plod up the Amazon with his Jungle Studs club, while Eddie kept himself to himself (and his wife Valerie) at his LA studio with engineer Donn Landee. It was here that he'd come up with the synth-based riff to 'Jump' some two years previously. He'd played it to the band then and they'd given it a blank, this time he was determined that they would do it.

"It was all because I was supposed to be guitar hero Joe Bitch, and keyboards didn't fit with the image or something. I disagreed with that and this time I decided just to do it."

Eddie, then and now, has always kept very quiet about the arguments that surrounded the music, the rows that led to the completion of *'1984'*. "The

• *'Get thee behind me, Roth!'* The US, the eighties.

music is all it boils down to," he said. "I get frustrated because there's so many things I just want to get out. I don't give a fuck if they sell, if people like it or not, I just want to get it out of me."

That was the standard line that Eddie reiterated in '84, along with the confession that he was "actively discouraged" from playing on outside projects. Quincy Jones was an exception. Here, for the first time, the paths divided, briefly and historically, between Eddie and Dave. Quincy was producing Michael Jackson's *Thriller* album, and wanted a guitar solo for 'Beat It'. There are several versions of the tale. In one, by far the best, Quincy chanced a call to Eddie's home, only to get a bad line and a guitarist who didn't know who he was or what he wanted. Insults were exchanged and the line went dead. Quincy rang again and got the message through — "Would you play the solo on 'Beat It'?" Eddie agreed, did the business without accepting a fee or any royalties, said a passing "Hello" to Michael Jackson and went back to his own studio. Much later he got a 'Thank you' telegram from Quincy Jones. It was signed "Quincy, The Jerk".

Whatever, that solo was a breakthrough. The guitar was unmistakeable, and it took Michael Jackson into crossover status in the USA; right on to white rock radio and all the way to Number One in the singles chart. Unratified rumour even had it for a while that some white rock stations were *only* playing the solo.

Eddie predictably played (no pun intended) the whole thing down, even to the point of feigning embarrassment at the fuss in some later interviews. "I don't see any way it could have hurt Van Halen; if anything it helped us, but I didn't do it for that reason either. I just did it for the goddamn fun. I like to play and sometimes it's sickening to have no-one to play with."

He didn't do it for the money either, or the fame. Eddie still sticks by his story that he didn't even know who Quincy Jones was until his father told him. And as for Michael Jackson? "He's a great guy. He came in and said 'I really like that high fast stuff you do' and went back to his ET, or whatever.

"I didn't want anything out of it, but maybe I'll need to take dancing lessons some day . . . I guess Michael owes me one!"

PHOTO: LFI

Eddie also took time out to play on Queen guitarist Brian May's 'Starfleet' project, but more crucially went back to the '5150' studio to hammer out the new ideas and styles that were to breathe life and fire into the 1984 Van Halen.

There could have been friction, cracks, a split. After all mid-1983 could have been seen as the peak, and with the average age of Van Halen rolling inexorably on towards the 30 mark, time to call it a day.

Instead, by curious and fortunate chronology, everything fell neatly into place. With barriers drawn up, lines established, the Edward versus David philosophy of Van halen — in essence the whole core of the success of *'1984'* (album and year up until the time of writing) — was first of all hammered out behind closed doors at the studio. David might have joked later: "Recording at Eddie's place was kind of easy, you know, sit back and have another beer and all that sort of thing" but it was a time of assessment, possibly even fierce rows. Yet with ten, eleven, nearly twelve years behind them the corporate might of Van Halen won the day.

By the time 'Beat It' was bulleting to the top, the album was in the can. By the time 'Jump' was pulled off the album for a post-Christmas firecracker single (which wasn't far behind 'Beat It' in hitting the top' the massive preparations for Van Halen's 'World Tour 1984' were all but completed.

And as for that friction? As in all good legends it was now "a guiding force", "the essence of Van Halen" — entirely legitimised and accepted (almost like saying 'You've been watching us all these years and you didn't *know* that?'). Slowly but surely brought out into the open it ended up as simple reasoning. Verbal jousting whereby Eddie laid it on the line and David hogged the headlines.

Van Halen were back on the road, and looking back it should have come as no surprise that the album gathered rave reviews (on *both* sides of the Atlantic), reached their highest Billboard slot to date (number two) and cemented all the glories achieved up until 1982. The American leg of the tour was sold out months in advance (as indeed had all their tours from 1979 until 1982), and in the first reports "awesome" was the word used most frequently to describe it. Then again, Van Halen's timing, whatever they had to put into it, was always impeccable.

'Jump' was a classic of its kind, indeed of any kind of pop song. A crossover hit (number one in the States by the end of January, number seven in Britain by February) and one that introduced Van Halen to a whole new audience — and the whole old audience to Eddie's subtle mastery of the synthesiser.

This time the message went out on video and on the airwaves. "The video will stay in touch with the Van Halen tradition," David proclaimed at the time. "We stay in touch with what's happening in the world. We read, we watch TV, and stay current. You may get big budget productions and big name directors, but in our own tradition we decided to make a video completely by ourselves and hand shoot it on a Super 8 camera.'' They did, and it got shown. And somewhere along the way the legend that started in 1976 gathered momentum. No matter that there were people all across the world buying up 'Jump' (and maybe later '1984') thinking that Van Halen had just arrived out of nowhere.

"This thing called Van Halen" had pulled itself out of the fire and was blasting its way across the world. At the beginning of the year David had taken on the old mantle of joker by saying: "I can tell you what 1984 means to me personally. At exactly a quarter to midnight on New Year's Eve I'm going to undo the buttons on my designer jeans with the Italian surname and loosen the string on my French sunglasses that you use for skiing and I'm going to plug in all my all-new waterproof headphones into my new state-of-the-art compact disc player and tune in my stereo hook-up to the cable channel that plays rock videos, and, at the stroke of twelve, I'm gonna aerobicise!''

Eddie had confined himself to the more succinct: "Whoever the bozo was who invented the clock can kiss my ass . . .''

By the end of the long hot summer they'd rumbled in triumph around America and finally made it to Europe by August, appearing as 'Special Guests' at the Castle Donington 'Monsters Of Rock Festival' in front of over 70,000 people on August 19. Second on the bill to AC/DC, they blasted and belted and cussed away . . . making the most of it. "They really enjoyed it, they thought the whole thing was a giggle,'' claimed a Warners aide afterwards. But this wasn't their own backyard, and, no, they didn't steal the show. Yet, somehow, it was enough.

There was still fuel left in the tank, and even if David's Kung Fu dancing and heavily camped up stage gymnastics, allied with the solo-they'd-come-to-

hear from Eddie (one critic even went so far as to dub them the Edward Van Halen Four; while the national press stuck to the David Lee Roth Mr Sexy tag) wasn't sufficient to create a premature holocaust, Van Halen emerged with honours even.

They hadn't come to prove themselves the best heavy metal band in the world — who needs those labels? They played and went away, back to the States. Object mission: complete. 1984 all but over, on stage at least.

The only thing that was certain on both sides of the Atlantic was that a message had been implanted that came over something like "stand by for further announcements . . . stand by for further announcements . . . stand by for further announcements . . .'' For the party was still very definitely going on. Like the Olympics in Los Angeles, Van Halen made a profit in 1984. More than a few people saw both. David even made the parallel when he was in the UK: "A Van Halen show is just like the Olympics, the 100 metre dash, followed by the shot putt.''

It could be they'll still be around for the next Olympics. Or they could do what Ronald Reagan is rumoured to be thinking of doing in two years time — retiring in mid-term of office. Whatever happens they've proved their worth.

Van Halen 1983–1984 . . . they who wait and win. They did it, they still are doing it. As David told *Sounds* magazine in August: "I don't care who's waiting for what. I don't feel any responsibility to the fans, record company, manager, agent or anyone. If I want to play any kind of music then I play it. I've been doing that since 1978.'' David also maintained that Van Halen would never sell out for record sales and never — "barring accidents of God or Ferrari" — call it a day.

We too, can only wait and wonder. Such are legends — especially when they might just be beginning.

8. David Lee Roth — Myth, Ms. and mastery

At the end of the day, all things considered, there would be no real notion of Van Halen if it wasn't for David Lee Roth. He's both the centre of the myth (in fact its *creator*) and the link between the Van Halen legend and reality.

Some critics argue that if it wasn't for one half of the brotherly duo born with the surname Van Halen — "Eddie the axeman" in short — there wouldn't be any music, any band, nothing. But it's always been Dave who's kept the Van Halen ball rolling, in a way quite unique amongst rock bands. He's set down the story for all to see, lived out the story for all to watch. Without his prognostications, his quotations, his brilliant summation of a lifestyle that probably (and I mean probably) only exists in the mind of Van Halen fans there would be no Van Halen.

Alex and Michael Anthony would qualify for walk-on parts in any heavy metal/hard rock scenario from 'Spinal Tap' to the real story of ZZ Top (if that ever gets written), but apart from propping up the odd bar stool and making not insignificant donations to the profits of Jack Daniels and Budweiser (Inc,) that's where their story ends.

And Eddie? So much of the Van Halen legend lies rooted in the wonderful "symbiosis" of this guitar genius and his loud-mouthed sidekick that nothing more needs to be added. For a man who once said: "I don't understand it, people change their musical styles like I change my underwear. I mean, I haven't changed my *hairstyle* in ten years. It's only music." He's let his role slip away from him. On the one hand he'll say to a reporter "Ask me anything you like, I'm an open book", and what you get is a history of guitar playing. On the other the message comes across loud and clear from the various aides and minders on both sides of the Atlantic — "Eddie rarely gives interviews". Shoot! Eddie rarely does anything but play the guitar. And he plays it with Van Halen. Full stop. If he's got any complaining to do (as Van Halen critics always infer that he has) he sure as hell doesn't do it in public. Not just yet anyway.

So it's back to good old reliable Dave, the surgeon's son from the Mid West. Creating rock 'n' roll reality out of rock 'n' roll banality and taking it back to the heartland. Getting the message across and making it stick. Without him there would be four characters and no story. Even the inestimable Mr Roth has admitted he's not the world's greatest singer. But he could have a fair claim to being one of rock's greatest

• *'I'm very happy by myself, I've never felt the need to live my life through another human being'* – DLR.

showmen, bar none. He created the Van Halen legend, appeared (to all intents and purposes) to live it to the full. Indeed he's still living it. Our debt (indeed my debt) to David Lee Roth is incalculable. As the Brits say, hats off to him!

In fact David Lee Roth (the aforementioned) lost his hat minutes after taking the stage at Castle Donington in Britain in August. It didn't worry him in the slightest — he wasn't *phased* as California speak might have it. He went out and did his best, Van Halen's best, the way he's been doing it since 1973.

In the flesh David Lee Roth isn't the "suntanned surfer, finely muscled, the essence of the Californian dream" as one scribe put it. He's an American rock star, take it or leave it.

He'll be hitting the thirty mark in less than a year from now, and although he's in "great physical shape" he's far from appearing the instant Adonis. "I

• *Donnington and Dave; monsters of rock wear hats (and lose them) and use real swords.*

like to live what we are, to give what we are," he once said. "Van Halen is sexy music, it makes me feel sexy. Why should I go out on stage spilling out over my belt buckle?"

Away from the stage he's shorter than you'd imagine. Aren't all rock stars like that? Think of Marley (RIP), Jagger, Springsteen, Dylan. Roth has that sort of status. But the famous "two foot mane of flowing blond hair that every girl would give her eye teeth for" is thinning ever so slightly. His eyes aren't as bright as they could be, and the teeth aren't those of a new young American. Until he talks, until you *see* the security, until you see him take the stage, he could be anybody. Joe Average with long hair and tight trousers (and there were plenty of those at Donington). American of course, who else would behave like that? But for all the visual faults David Lee Roth *is* Van Halen — the living, fucking, rocking, rolling legend.

Don't ask Eddie (even if he did once talk to Michael Jackson) just *listen* to David . . .

★★★★

Just about every interview with David Lee Roth starts off with a description about what it's like to interview David Lee Roth. The "motor mouth" with "verbal diarrhoea"; or as one hapless hack put it "interviewing David Lee Roth is like hitting the jackpot on a fruit machine — you stick your coin in and a great stream of verbiage comes spilling out".

In fact it's nothing of the sort. Legend has it that Dave huffs and puffs and shouts and makes jokes and laughs a lot. A lot of Americans do that, especially if they happen to be involved in rock 'n' roll. Van Halen's road crew for instance.

Instead reality has it that DLR is the best switch hitter ever to come out of the West Coast. His version of the Van Halen story is the one that is believed, and for some bizarre reason women journalists believe it more than even Dave does. Christ, and they're the ones that never even go to the concerts!

What follows is a brief glimpse at the sex and drugs and rock and roll (and the mega bucks that follow) image of Van Halen as espoused by one David Roth. It's worth mentioning that he remembers good lines for interviews a whole lot better than he remembers

lines of songs he's written, but that's all part of the fun.

On stage he's "pure energy" — or as the *Daily Mirror* put it "naughty gymnastics, cartwheels, back-flips and somersaults culminate in a Kung Fu sword fight — Mr Sexy should steal the show!" That was about the Donington dust up with AC/DC, and they didn't.

Off stage he's also "pure energy" ("He was the one guy who would always go out of his way to make a point, make an impression, get some kind of reaction," says Dave Jarrett, who handled Van Halen's press in the UK up until 1980. "David said something and you believed it.") and doggedly determined to plug the Van Halen message. In a sense he's got two jobs, and you'd have to admit — who's dared ask Dave? — that he does his second a whole better than his first. It's fun, fast and furious *talking* to David Lee Roth; not that many people who've done it have ever said the same thing about watching him perform. Take it or leave it, this guy calls the shots. And if you've read the quotations before, don't say you haven't been warned; stories always improve with a second telling.

★★★★

The early history of Van Halen has already been chronicled. Needless to say it *is* repeated in modern interviews — everything from "I was a hyperactive child" to "I used to do my Monkey Hour every night". Then there's the years in the bars in California, the years of success, right up to the most modern Van Halen/Roth cliché; "Van Halen will go on forever, barring accidents of God or Ferrari". (OK, so that's now the fifth time you've heard it!). And while a lot of the Van Halen story has been earnestly laid down by male "critics" in the States and male "fan critics" in the UK, it should come as no surprise that the best material — from Dave's and Van Halen's point of view — usually comes when he's interviewed by women.

As early as 1980 David was describing all rock critics as Elvis Costello. "They all like him in the States because they all look like him," he said, and the taunt was repeated at countless concerts across America, usually with the added barb that while the critics went home and sat behind their typewriter with Costello on the compact disc player, their kids were upstairs getting out of it with Van Halen on the headphones of their Sony Walkman. He was probably right.

But faced with the likes of Kristine McKenna (already mentioned) and Diana Clapton of *Oui* magazine in the States, Ros Russell, Paula Yates (of Fleet Street and TV fame in the UK), Robbi Millar of *Sounds* magazine, and latterly (and most surprisingly) Fiona Russell Powell of the highly influential "young styles, young trends" glossy mag *The Face*, Dave plays ball and gets to the heart of the matter. "I like to look at interviews as a conversation," he said once, and has said often since. "It's interesting, it's a challenge, an exchange of views. We should both go away having got something out of it."

To make a massive generalisation (and isn't that just typical of Van Halen?) the guys talk to Dave and wish they were talking to Eddie about music. They think they have better jokes than the blond maestro (they never have), or that they have a better way of writing down how Dave talks (they never do either). The girls ask the questions, and get the legend taped.

For instance (from an interview with *The Face*) — *The Face:* "You once said that every woman that wanted you, got you. Is that really true?" David: "Absolutely. Why? Do you want me? You only have to ask . . .'

Or (from *Sounds*) — *Sounds:* "Do you ever have any problems with women?" David: "Yeah, exploding women!" *Sounds:* "What do you mean?" David: "A girl gets back stage wearing something really tight and you say 'How did ya get into that?' Explode!"

And so the legend rolls on. Dave the stud, but one who always denies that Van Halen are sexist and always gets away with it. He's capable of switching from the outrageous to the implacably calm and reasoned mode of "conversation". After all it is his life's work. "I play the instrument I have", he told *Oui*, in an oblique reference to the display of his Spandex covered anatomy on stage. But he plays it all ways — a body with a brain.

David Lee Roth is the most effective advertisement for a rock band ever to have come out of America. Other groups copy Van Halen in all sorts of ways, but other groups don't have Dave. He's got the philosophy, the commitment, the look and the lyrics. And even if he wouldn't be where he is today without the help of three others who also happen to be in Van Halen it's him who's made them top dogs.

● *'OK, I can make you believe anything I want'*.

The Face called him a "24 hour person" — Dave'll get people to believe anything. And when they got to the heart of the matter up popped Dave with his usual precise summation. "The press talk a lot about sex with Van Halen; every third question is about that. I know I talk about it a lot but you see I like being open about it and Van Halen's music makes me feel very sexy.

"I'm one of the architects, so when I hear it, it makes me feel sexy all over again, and when we play it, I get even sexier.

"I'm a total enthusiast. Everyone has to participate in what Dave's doing. It's been like that since I was a young kid and now I do it for a living."

The perfect mixture. Jim Dandy for looks, Huckleberry Finn (one of his new heroes) for enthusiasm, a cold-blooded assessment of what he's in it for and why he's in it that would do any businessman or politician proud, and the end result — a credible rock star. "Reality is what you make it," said Dave. "If I live it, create it, breathe it, then that's reality, right? That's rock stardom, it's everything!"

"Do you think you're Captain America?" asked The Face. "Yeah I am, and obnoxiously proud of it," replied Dave. And just this once he didn't mention Van Halen.

The man, after all, is a master and a myth maker. He's taken Van Halen to the top ("we're worth millions and millions of dollars, I don't even know how much") and intends them to stay there. He might leave you with the rock clichés like "as we say in the music business, here today, gone later today" but he touches the right chords in the right places; playing the instrument he has, if you like.

And, at the last count, he's only been doing it for thirty years so far . . .

PHOTO: LFI

9. Until the next time...

The final part of the Van Halen story is really a debunking of yet another American myth — one that runs roughly along the lines that 'in order for a writer or artist to achieve greatness he (or she) must be either neurotic or possessed of a fatal flaw'.

Van Halen are the exception in every way so far. "I hate to disappoint anyone but I'm normal," Eddie once said. This, from the "world's greatest rock 'n' roll guitarist".

And, as for that word "greatest"? "I don't know where Van Halen are going to go down in history," David told Laura Canyon in a recent interview. "You can't be concerned with making history. In fact history is often made long after the fact, when people are made heroes, shining examples of something or other.

"We're not concerned. It's our life and times. You go out and do things and then you distill it into a piece of plastic and you sell it people. That is what we do.

- *'I think . . . therefore I play'*.

That's not greatness and that's not making history."

Instead it's just hard work and good fortune, that grand old American dream. And rip-offs and stumbling blocks and obligations and image. But that's part of the American dream too, ever since the Mafia, the movies, the wars, Watergate and finally even old Reagan himself.

But sociology hour ended in Southern California when David, Eddie, Alex and Michael met up all those years ago. Since then they've been running with the dollar. David with his laughs (he always *laughs* in interviews, the story has it) and his leaps, Eddie with his fingers and his fretboards. No neurosis here, no fatal flaws. Van Halen are simply a group, a very successful rock 'n' roll group. By 1984 they'd transcended a vast body of common belief and folklore and become the biggest rock group in America.

On the way their combativeness and chemistry has been scrutinised from the outside, the external bones laid bare. Some of the disparity, briefly summarised, follows.

PHOTO: LFI

But at the time of writing they're still a group and if David Lee Roth still chooses to say things (as he did recently) like: "I can see Van Halen going on for several more decades. We're a lot better now, playing tighter, getting along better. Having lots of fun" there's less and less people out there inclined to disbelieve him.

There's bonding and interdependence in Van Halen, not so much the gentle tugging of opposite ends of the magnet, rather the locking of horns amidst a vast cacophony of noise, ego and creativity. "We have fabulous arguments," Dave told *Circus* magazine. "You couldn't get any more opposite. But somehow the chemistry works. "People always think because you're in a band there's some sort of tribal rigmarole where you all hang out beating the same drum to the same rhythm. That's nonsense. It's

● *'People change styles like I change my underwear'* – *Edward Van Halen.*

much better to have differing opinions and bounce ideas around."

The chemistry of Van Halen is something David Lee Roth understands down to the last detail. He takes it in his stride when Eddie states (as he did to David Fricke): Alex and I are the real Van Halen. Without us there couldn't be Van Halen. There could always be a band without Dave. And I write all the music." He *knows*, because Eddie follows it up by looking around a 30,000 seater at the soundcheck and saying: "But if there was no Dave it would be pretty empty here tonight. They're both entertainment, just different kinds. It all adds up to releasing a lot of anxieties for people." Not least of all Edward Van Halen.

Dave's lines are conversely all-embracing, uttered more often, easier to penetrate. Things like "We all have our own abilities. What Eddie can do I could never aspire to. And vice versa." Or "Most of what I've learned about music I've learned from Edward and Alex. I'm a lot better at dancing than I am at singing. Edward and Alex haven't learned to dance yet. But we're working on it." Or even: "You'd never get Edward Van Halen hosting a chat show!"

And of course, David writes all the lyrics. In many ways he wrote the whole story. Beholden to nobody, but inexorably linked to Van Halen. Without him you'd never believe that Van Halen were "four distinct personalities". At least he never claims that Van Halen is more than sum of its parts, that wonderful British rock cliché (and anyway on stage it's usually only Dave's that are visible). Without him, it seems at times, the whole Van Halen circus would have ended before it started — as a forgotten dream somewhere in the back room of a bar somewhere in Santa Barbara.

He can get away with his standard slag-off of Eddie's solo on 'Beat It' ("I heard the original tape of 'Beat It' and it was abominable. Michael was lucky he got Edward on the case. But he didn't do nothing new — he just went and played the same fucking solo he's been playing with us for ten years. Michael Jackson does a heavy metal song, so he gets the best heavy metal guitarist in. Big deal! Where was the change?") as well as withstanding the ravages of time and his loudly declared abuse of himself. Narrator and show-

• *Eddie throws his axe (above) while David 'interacts with his audience on a socio-cultural level' (right).*

man, self-styled star of the fairy tale. Believe it or not. He does. He also knows that Edward (in particular), Alex and Michael Anthony wrote the soundtrack, that he might fall to earth like a bird without wings if it wasn't for Van Halen, and that right now he's not even going to give it a try. Yessir, we still have a Van Halen party on our hands, courtesy of California, Warner Brothers and everybody who ever came along to watch, listen, marvel or simply hate. And that's a lot of people.

It's the sort of shindig that doesn't suddenly stop when you ask Dave a dumbo question like 'What will you be doing in twenty years time?' ("Walking, I hope") or 'How do you keep yourself so fit? ("Doing tongue push-ups"). For once, even, it's not too late to join in. The moral is enjoy or stay away, and give up all that garbage about "deeply sensitive artists". Turn it up . . . or turn off.

Within their own strictly defined parameters and their own self-created legend (of which this whole slim volume is merely an outline) Van Halen are as happy as pigs in shit. "It's important to remember that success is never final and failure is never fatal," said Dave. "But the most important part is that it's not whether you win or lose, it's how good you looked!" Or even how you sounded.

As this book was being completed it was announced that Michael Jackson had accepted a multi-million dollar offer to make a full length feature film based on the making of 'Beat It'. There hasn't been a whisper yet about who's been invited, but don't count on it spoiling the Van Halen bash.

It's always said that rock 'n' roll bands don't change the course of history — they merely make their own (and even the cocooned and invincible Michael Jackson can't do anything about that). This is Van Halen's . . . until the next time.

It's also a bit of America's too, along with Big Macs, big mouths from the heartland, successful second generation immigrants and that whole desire to be top of the heap. "You've got to roll with the punches, and get to what's real", as David sang in 'Jump'.

Never let it be said that Van Halen never lived out their own clichés.